ADVENT PRESENCE

ADVENT PRESENCE

Kissed by the Past, Beckoned by the Future

MELFORD "BUD" HOLLAND

Morehouse Publishing
NEW YORK

Morehouse Publishing, 19 East 34th Street, New York, NY 10016

Morehouse Publishing is an imprint of Church Publishing Incorporated.
www.churchpublishing.org

Cover design by Laurie Klein Westhafer
Typeset by PerfecType, Nashville, TN

Library of Congress Cataloging-in-Publication Data
Holland, Melford "Bud".
  Advent presence : kissed by the past, beckoned by the future / Melford "Bud" Holland.
     pages cm
  Includes bibliographical references.
  ISBN 978-0-8192-3217-5 (pbk.) — ISBN 978-0-8192-3218-2 (ebook)
  1. Advent. 2. Devotional literature. I. Title.
  BV40.H645 2015
  242'.332—dc23

                              2015012932

Printed in the United States of America

Dedication

To my parents, Melford and Hilda Holland, and my sister,
Nancy, who have loved me beyond my wildest imagining,
encouraged me to ask questions, and valued me in ways that
will always feed my spirit.

To my wife, Annie, who has journeyed with me in the vineyard in life-giving and loving ways as a wonderful companion
to me and mother to our children, Craig, Eric, and Amanda.

To all the people who have graced my midst over the years
in so many ways. I continue to discover who I am because of
all of these wonderful people—past, present, and future—
who are fellow sojourners along my present paths and the
paths to come.

Contents

Introduction

I invite you to enter holy space, holy ground, and to redeem the time. Advent is a season that can be twenty-two to twenty-eight days long, a time when the present moment is kissed by the past while it beckons us to the future. In this sense it is like all other days and seasons, but in this moment we are reminded that life presents itself in split seconds of time, awaiting our observation and visions. Responding to the ever ancient, ever new questions of life that come full circle to us in Advent, the reflections within these pages look through the lens of our human experiences while connecting to our tradition, culture, and strongly held personal positions. Every moment offers the possibility of new pictures of creation, struggle, redemption, justice and injustice, and mystery, which expands our imagination, breaks our hearts, and offers hope and insights.

I invite you to enter this season of Advent and to explore the depths and breadth of life in its complexities. We are a people of the context, a people of the gathering, a people of the table, and a people of the dismissal. As a people of the context we experience the full range of human emotions and life experiences. In our gatherings we reach out for a community of persons and our connection with all creation as we enter a space that seeks to draw out our deepest yearnings in life. The tables of our life are many, including the holy table of a religious community, tables where we gather for conversations and meaning making, platforms where we crouch down with loved ones and strangers to share a vision of life itself and glimpses of promise. As tempting as it might feel to stay at the table, we are dismissed yet again to journey into the contexts of our living where life in its fullness and variability awaits.

I am involved in the Education for Ministry (EfM)[1] program as a trainer and have been informed over the years by the intersection of human experience, tradition (including scripture), culture, and personal positions as sources of authority, along with a myriad of voices that seek to contribute to the definition of who we are and what we might do. Advent is the season where these sources most intensively clash. We are drawn by a culture to the pressures of the pre-Christmas season often without reference to the birth of Christ; pulled by our personal positions, which hold our deep values and memories born in yesteryear about this time; informed by scripture and tradition that not only points to the past but also to the future coming of Christ while wondering what is that birth of Christ we want to be born in us today. We experience these powerful influencers in our lives as we seek to juggle the demands on our time today, all the while wondering what are the most important issues and questions we need to ask on our journey at this time.

As I wrote these reflections, it became an opportunity to look at Advent preparation with a different set of lenses, questions, and concerns from within our common human experience, including our spiritual, emotional, physical, and mental labor. In my teaching there are a series of questions I often get asked in various forums, meetings, gatherings, and contexts. Asked in different ways, they each have subsets of questions—questions of identity, relationship, inclusion, vocation, mission, work, and evaluation. You will find these questions sprinkled throughout these days of Advent, each one offering a doorway or window to other questions. They act as *cairns* (carefully placed rocks serving as markers) along the pathways of our living while illuminating and guiding the trail.

I hosted a collection of pictures for Advent in 2013 under the work of the Episcopal Church and the Visual Arts (ECVA). In an invitation to photographers who might share pictures depicting Advent themes, I shared some of the following thoughts. The word Advent is derived from the word *adventus,* which means coming. Life stands still for a millisecond but also brings to that moment the memories of our past and the anticipation of the future. Carrying a camera is one way of reflecting on life in those moments in a different way. So can our quickened prayers, conversations, and reflections gathered in myriads of ways. Our journeys might take us to the heartaches of social injustice, the promise of a fuller life for those around us, or the radical hospitality afforded by people and creation itself. Resources and pictures can fill us up, as we need to take steps into the future.

What might be your pictures and images? What images might be helpful for you to put into your satchel or knapsack as you contemplate your future journeys through Advent? What stories come to mind? What stories would you like to tell? They can range from incredible images of our creation, the inter-section where hands are extended in love and friendship, and how smiles and encouragement are randomly and wonderfully offered. Stories can come from times when reconciliation and healing are expressed. They can describe times when we wit-ness or experience the willingness to stand in the whirlwinds of life with others in celebration or in times when our hearts are broken. Advent can come in a whole host of ways to you.

Advent is that season where we especially view life simul-taneously from the perspectives of the past, present, and future. From those positions we can see that life in other sea-sons and times can also take on that same full journey. It is that place where your reflected experience might invite you into the space where the present moment meets memories of the past and imagines future hope. This is the place of new birth, generativity, and creativity. It is such a small moment in time, but promises to be sufficient and life giving.

I invite you to experience all measures of reflections and explorations of the most important questions of our lives. The reflections that follow for each day of Advent encompass a broad range of experiences and stories, including photography, social service, teaching, healing, and community building on many levels—all of which, along with countless other examples of work, take us to the depths of our spirituality, the breadths of conversation and reflections, and to heights of hope and promise. My hope is that they will lead you to self-examination, observations of the broader communities of our humanity, and to value the insights that are spawned by our human experience. Advent leads us back to God, who seems to call us again and again into being vessels of God's grace, love, forgiveness, reconciliation, and healing.

I invite your readiness to reflect on your human experience as we begin this sacred journey of Advent—a time to remember, to be reminded, and to be surprised.

Bud Holland
February 2015

Beginnings
Where Are We?

Patience

I welcome you to a holy journey in these weeks ahead. On this First Sunday of Advent, we hear the call for patience. Our Gospel reading for today from Luke 21 evokes a sense of hope and anticipation as we await the "Son of Man coming in a cloud with great glory" (v. 27). Jesus assures us (v. 35) that the day will come for everyone in which the scriptures will be fulfilled; the whole cosmos will be involved in redemption. We need to "Be alert at all times" (v. 36), which requires great patience.

Advent is a time of re-creating an old sacred journey. The setting aside of these days was an attempt as early as the third century to prepare yet again for the coming of Christ in our hearts. What does it mean that God sent God's Son into the world to be born in human flesh? How might we take some time to reflect on this incredible gift and lay again the foundation to receive this truth into the fabric of our lives, the crevices of our souls and spirits, and the life-blood of our bodies? It is in the experience of Advent that we can open ourselves to be yet again surprised by the joy of birth and to see that this birth is about another birthing within us. Let us look at each day of Advent to see ways our daily living intersects with the joyful, hopeful expectation of this birth, and how this birth is already presenting itself in the way we view life, ask questions, and contemplate life's persistent challenges.

Many years ago I experienced heart arrhythmia. It happened unexpectedly on a Sunday morning just as I was awakening from sleep. After an extensive checkup, nothing was found that could have caused that condition to materialize. Over the next few years it occurred on other occasions at the same time of day with the same checkup and results. While it has been ten years since the last episode, one of the gifts of those occurrences is that I welcome each new day with great gratitude. Today is a gift beyond measure. What might I do, be, accomplish, try on, explore, or give thanks for on this day?

In the Christian calendar, this first day of Advent is the beginning of a new year. For some of us our hearts can be pounding with anticipated meetings and deadlines. They also may be pounding with excitement about seeing an old friend or anticipated time with a family member. Or perhaps this day reminds us of a loss or worry that can sometimes envelop our hearts, breaking them yet again and again. Advent can also be a time when we remember our histories and recall when a yearning for a messiah was on the lips of many and a hoped-for rescue from bondage was sought. Who is the messiah for whom we wish? What might happen if the messiah becomes present? So what seems like a split second, our present-moment thoughts might welcome both past and future hope.

As tempted as we might be to draw conclusions, jump into the future, or make something happen, today we can pause and wait for something to happen in our hearts, our prayers, our spirits, our relationships, and our observations of the world around us and within us. For many of us this is becoming increasingly hard to do. There is so much that can cause us fear, anxiety, and impatience to want to make something happen. Perhaps we might choose to follow a different path if only for a little while today and over the next few weeks. It just might make all the difference in what we observe.

When I worked in New York City, I often stayed in the City because it was easier than tackling the commute (two to two-and-a-half hours each way). But when I did go to Penn Station for my train, I often noticed the crowds increasing and the pace of walking quicken the closer I came to the station. By the time I got to the stairs or escalator, it was a mad rush. I often wondered why I and others were paying the price for someone else being late for the train as they were rushing and pushing to get to the track. Of course, I was on occasion that person myself. Where did patience go in this picture? The same is true on the road as cars hug our bumpers, drivers honk at us at every turn, and at the end of a run as we are stopped yet again I notice there are only a few cars ahead.

After 9/11 there was a strange silence in the City for several weeks. I heard no horns being blown. Yes, there were many sirens of emergency vehicles, but little or no sounds from other drivers. There seemed to be a moment of respect, giving way, and patience in our collective suffering and shock that honored the fact that we needed to go into an interior space to come to some initial terms with what had happened to us in our external world. After time, the noise and impatience returned, but the memory of that earlier time is always within me. It gives me hope that people can rise to the occasion, on occasion, and offer space for others to grieve, integrate, and reflect on their lives.

The yearning for the coming of a Messiah was palpable in the hundreds of years leading up to the birth of Jesus of Nazareth. The Jews felt assured that God would not abandon them. They also believed that God was active in history so that historical events took on special significance for them. These hopes were ignited even more with the revolt of Judas Maccabeus in the middle of the second century BCE, and were both challenged and heightened further after the Romans took over the land 100 years later.

So we may sing on this day: O Come, O Come Emmanuel. We are in the present moment, kissed by the past, and being beckoned to the future.

Reflect

1. What might your experience of patience and impatience have to say about what is brewing inside your life and spirit?
2. How can we keep our impatience at bay just long enough to stand in the whirlwind of these questions and be present to a new birth just waiting to be birthed within us?
3. How can the Christ that we yearn for be born again and again in our hearts?

Questions

As I connect with individuals and groups, I hear many important questions. Some of the recurring questions are these: Who am I? Who are you? Who are we? Whose are we? Who is the "we" that we yearn to be? What is our task/vocation/mission in life? How do we proceed? How do we know we are proceeding? Are we there yet? These are the most important questions of our lives.

We live in a world of complex contexts. That is saying the obvious, but it is even more complex than we can imagine. I remember growing up in a little village in West Virginia. Our fathers and some mothers worked for the company that owned our homes, had a grocery story, sponsored the Little League baseball teams, offered a summer camp, and hosted an outing at an amusement park once a year. When I was in elementary school, we moved several times on the same street. We were all in the same economic class; we lived in segregated housing and communities in those early years. On the surface it seemed fairly predictable. The crime rate was virtually nonexistent. There was some bootlegging going on and more than occasional fights with other guys. But there was also a lot of pulling together and being proud of being West Virginians.

My family was small in one sense: father, mother, sister, and myself. But it was huge in other ways: twenty-one first cousins grew up in that village as my parents' families settled there to work at the plant or in the mines. There were large numbers of children there in proportion to the overall population. All of us lived around a road, a railroad track, a river, and the mountains. One could drive down Route 60 and think that life was on an even keel and not very complex. Yet it was far from simple or predictable.

Complexities came in many ways: the levels of segregation and racism that were persistent in the valley as with other communities; the layers of management in the plants and mines that were seen as inherently unfair; the pollution of the plants (the valley had the highest percentage of death by cancer in the whole country); the resources that were stripped from the land and taken out of state; economic stagnation; and the families with young children who had moved elsewhere. I came to realize that our life was complex and difficult on many fronts when our family visited my grandparents about forty miles away. I would ascend the hillside above town and look down into the valley. Both venues offered some opportunities to reflect in new ways.

From this small segment of reality to the much larger pictures of a global village, we know that our lives are complex beyond our full understanding. We are pulled in many directions with many voices seeking to tell us who we are. This reality becomes intensified in the Advent season where life around us quickens and the pace of decision making on many levels is breathtaking.

It may be especially appropriate in this first week of Advent to engage in the following questions: Who am I? Who are you? Who are we together? Whose are we (who do we belong to)? Who is the "we" that we yearn to be? What is our vocation, mission, or task in life? How do we proceed with our lives? How do we know we are moving forward? And are we there yet? These questions are identity questions, relational questions, mission and direction of life questions, evaluative questions, and wondering questions. The questions, though separate, intertwine with one another and form a new mosaic from which to enter this journey again. They are indeed life questions.

One of the questions young children ask is, "Why?" How often did I brush by this question with my children by saying, "Because I said so" or "Why not?" Questions can feel irritating, yet they offer a window into others' thinking and new ground for exploration. In my early years when I began to think, foolishly, that I had many of the answers to life's persistent questions, I learned that I did not.

"Why did God allow my son to die?" This question has haunted me for many years since I was asked it at the bedside of a young boy who died so unexpectedly and so young. I responded, "I do not know. But I do believe that God loves your son and all of us more than we can imagine." I believe that to be true. We don't have all the answers for sure. We live in mystery, hope, faith, and a willingness (or not) to stand in the whirlwind of life ourselves and with others. Questions beget questions.

Sometimes there is another way of relating without questions and that has to do with feelings and what we sense is going on within us and within others. Now that I am getting older I hear myself asking yet again, "Why?"

Scripture is filled with questions. Perhaps the most repeated verses in the Bible have to do with fear. Be not afraid. May we be not so afraid that we might be open to the questions, the feelings, and the senses of life happening around and between us. May we take the time to seize the day and explore it to the fullest. It just may make all the difference.

Reflect

1. Who are you? Whose are you?
2. Who do you long to be?
3. What are the most compelling questions of your life?

Déjà Vu

The beginning of Advent focuses on the ministry of John the Baptist. The Gospel of Luke places John's ministry in its context in history and reminds us that the prophet Isaiah had foretold that John would come to prepare the way of the Lord. Part of the preparation John brought was a call to conversion, a call to turn in a new direction. This radical call guides our preparation for a new day.

I remember taking our oldest son on a college exploration trip. It was a wonderful experience and one replicated with our other children. As we drove through one town he said, "I have just had a Vujà dé experience." Now he was very bright and gifted in speech. I tenderly said to him, "You must have meant a Déjà vu experience." "No," he says, "a Vujà dé experience."

18

I then said, "Okay, what is a Vujà dé experience?" He replied, "I am sure that I have never had this experience of seeing this town before." We laughed and drove on thinking that indeed he had passed in many ways.

We come to Advent with both a Déjà vu and Vujà dé experience. On the one hand we have been here before, even if we have not recognized that it was Advent. It is the time of the preparation for Christmas, that rushed time between Thanksgiving and Christmas, that hurtles us toward a known and unknown experience; a time when we (in the Northern Hemisphere) begin to sense a chill in the air. It is the season when college football goes into bowl mode, basketball begins to flourish, professional football gets close to deciding who will be in the playoffs, Christmas decorations occupy our common space and homes, Congress goes on a long vacation, and some movies are rushed into distribution to make the cut for consideration of future awards (and to reap monetary benefits of a holiday showing). The list could go on and on. It is a rhythm that is out of our control, yet one in which we have some control regarding how it affects us. Yet even in its yearly predictability it comes to us ever new. We live a life that is both Déjà vu and Vujà dé.

Advent is such a Déjà vu and Vujà dé experience. The biblical readings circle back round every three years to catch our hearing just enough to know we have heard them before, and yet are fresh enough to meet us in a new place of hearing. The story line is the same with some variances. The issue of balancing a yearned-for time for reflection and meditation with the internal drive to replicate patterns and customs of years gone by pull and push us toward competing "wants." We might feel driven and want to retreat at the same time. It is a time when we look forward, look backward, and look down to see what ground we are standing upon. In this regard it mimics life at its depth and breadth as much as any season. What is our life about, we might ask—it is about living Advent.

Advent, that season where we are kissed by the past, beckoned by the future, and drawn to our present moments, is now in its third day. It is Tuesday, that non-descript day of the week that seems to have no other tag on it. Mondays—we either love them or hate them. Many now call Wednesdays "hump days" where we cross over the beginning of a work-week and begin thinking about the freedom of a weekend. A new trend in social media is to call Thursdays "Throwback Thursdays," as a time to remember the past by sharing pictures of years gone by. Fridays are the entrance to a weekend and as such bring a new step to our walk. And then there are Tuesdays. What do you make of this Tuesday in your life?

Tuesday has such a mixed review in our history. The name *Tuesday* derives from the Old English *Tiwesdæg* and literally means "Tiw's Day" from the Old English word for god or deity. In some Slavic languages the word Tuesday originated from a word meaning "the second." In the Eastern Orthodox Church, Tuesdays are dedicated to John the Baptist.

With such a variation of meanings, what meaning do we want to attach to this Tuesday? Can we connect them to God, or a "turning around" as John the Baptist calls us to?

The beauty of life is that we are often given the opportunity to name something, redefine a circumstance, and embrace the possibilities that life brings. Such is the opportunity for us today. How might we see the extraordinary within the ordinary, the possibility of forgiveness within the woundedness, hope within despair, laughter within foibles, creation within destruction, welcome within loneliness, hospitality within shunning, or openness within judgment?

Tuesday can be a day when we can come to terms that we are within a work week and we can either be chagrined by it or embrace it. In a way it represents life without other tags. We might feel at times that we are like John the Baptist, crying in the wilderness, but we can remember that John chose that way of life for himself—a life of repentance (turning around) and a life that pointed to a greater life that was coming into the world.

A number of years ago a friend visited with me just after Easter. He shared a couple of things that I have never forgotten. He said, "I wish you would slow down a bit as you passed average a long time ago." After both of us paused, he added, "I have two bits of good news to share with you. The Messiah has come. And you are not the one!" I can be so driven (even in my laid back way) that I believe life around me is so important for me to affect that I can lose perspective of where I am and who I am.

Tuesday holds promise to be a day where we see ourselves realistically. And as we do we can see that we too do not have to be "messiahs," yet each one of us is extraordinary in our own right. There has never been someone like you and there never will be again.

May your day be filled with Déjà vu and Vujà dé experiences.

Reflect

1. Today might be a time to begin keeping a journal during Advent to record your thoughts and feelings, new sightings and insights, and identify yet more questions you would like to explore. What should be written today?
2. When have you felt like John the Baptist, crying in the wilderness? What would your cry be today?
3. When you have had such experiences, how did you feel and what did you learn?

The Present of Presence

A few years ago a friend of mine and I shared a couple of beers, hamburgers, and fries in a restaurant along the Hudson River in New York City. The scenery was wonderful. I remember it was a little cool but still comfortable. The conversation was a gift, even greater than the meal. I always enjoyed the times that Rick would come into the City; we both approached learning in similar ways. Our sharing of ideas often expanded our imaginations and brought new perspectives on life itself.

As we exited the restaurant to make our way back to our lodging just east of Union Square, we met a homeless man named Larry. I remember shaking his hand and sharing some introductions. Larry was hopeful for some money, so I reached into my pocket and retrieved a few dollars. As I was doing this I realized that Larry had the greasiest hand I had ever shaken. We talked a little more and then Rick and I made our way east through the Manhattan sunshine, eager to get an ice cream cone. But it occurred to me, "How can we eat an ice cream cone when our hands are so greasy?" Finding a public rest room for those just walking through the streets of New York City is not easy, however; we located a pharmacy that had some hand sanitizer and bottled water. As we stopped at the corner of Avenue of the Americas and 14th Street to wash our hands over a drainage grate in the street, we realized that we did not want to wash our hands from our encounter with Larry. How can we wash our hands and still hold Larry in our hands and in our memory?

We are inextricably connected to every human being on the planet. At this time of Advent we look back to reflect on all who have gone before, wonder about future connections with families and friends, and then think about what we are to do, can do, and should do with the strangers who come into our midst. Rick and I concluded our hand washing and found an ice cream store on 14th Street. Our conversations then deepened in new directions regarding who is our neighbor.

As we journey into Advent we also are invited to journey with the poorest, weakest, and most abused members of the human family. Elizabeth O'Connor reflects on this in her article, *Marks of a Liberating Community*.[2] As followers of Jesus, we are called to look for Christ in the most unlikely places: among the poor and needy, with those who break with convention and seek out new lifestyles, with the very persons whom the "real world" considers of no account. O'Connor speaks of the gifts received by communities (and individuals) when we are committed to the poor, a life of dialogue, critical contemplation, reflection, and solitude.[3] In the history of our traditions, we often find at its core people who connected with others whom were often discarded or unnamed in our world.

Having been connected over the years with people who were living on the margins of our society, I often see that they have become part of my life. Each of them has a name and a history. The hidden histories behind their faces and in their hearts could break our hearts. They are on the edge of survival, consistently vulnerable to external threats, and often are severely depressed.

At this point in Advent we are beginning to think about presents we might buy for others. I invite you to embrace the present in which you are living; in that embrace you might just experience the presents that keep on giving through a lifetime.

Reflect

1. What is the most special present you would like to give?
2. What is the present you would especially like to receive?
3. How might you be present (physically, spiritually, emotionally) to others during this season of Advent?

A New Start

A number of years ago my family and I experienced a terrible tragedy. My uncle was murdered and my aunt was severely beaten. Our collective grief was overwhelming. We were angry, but especially we were so very sad. As we gathered for the burial service for my uncle, we had a prayer service and home Eucharist for our family. At that Eucharist we also prayed for the three men who did this awful deed. As I sought to get my mind around how I might pray for all of these men, I began to realize that I could pray that they have a new start. I may never be with them along the way, but I hoped they would have a new start with an accepted accountability for their misdeeds with possible growth into a greater maturity, responsibility, and health in the years to come. This wishing for a new start for the other has been helpful to me in the years since. I have come to understand that forgiveness involves many rooms in our houses of memory and that perhaps wishing a new start for them is like entering the foyer of that house.

Advent is a time to contemplate God's wish to give us a new start. It is God's most precious gift of his Son that signals the new start. Phillips Brooks, noted preacher and writer of the nineteenth century, once told the story of a man who experienced a new start in a surprising way. He had refused yet again to go to the Christmas Eve service with his family and settled into the warmth of his home on a cold, blustery night. He noticed a flock of birds seeking to get into his barn in order to flee the ferocity of the wind. They had obvious difficulty in locating the entrance. The man thought to himself, if he could become a bird, he could fly ahead of them and lead them into the barn. Then he knew what Christmas was all about. He put on his boots and heavy jacket and joined his family at the service. Sometimes we get our clue about the meaning of life and God's love through nature and the unexpected.

One of our life questions is: Do we want a new start for ourselves? And, if we do, what would that look like? As we contemplate God's gift of his Son to us, we may understand it by contemplating these questions and "new starts."

Creation occurred billions of years ago, and the evolving life that is earth, stars, and universes has spans of time that boggle our imagination. In more recent history, God continually offered a new start to people who did not live up to the covenant with God. A "new start" is at the core of life itself when every breath we take is a new breath; everyone we forgive (including ourselves) is creating a new start for themselves as well as for us; and every confession, declaration of vision, extension of handshakes, and offering of peace is actualizing the possibility of a new start. Change is inevitable, but growth isn't. Life without change is death. We have an opportunity to grow as human beings as we embrace the reality of change in our life, seeking the new starts afforded to us in our living. A new start can be for us a belief that God has not given up on us. Our responsibility is to remain open to the possibility of that new start and try not to build a wall around ourselves to protect us from that new start occurring.

Advent is a good time to review our religious traditions to see how new starts have been expressed and experienced by our ancestors. At various times of the year, including between Christmas and New Year's Day, the families on my mother's side would gather at my grandparents' home. It was there that I heard the stories of my ancestors and learned to appreciate the gift of storytelling and my heritage. We would eat a sumptuous dinner of chicken and dumplings with even more sumptuous conversation in the living room.

When I was a young boy it seemed to me that the living room was huge, only to discover years later how small it was in size. Yet the struggles, celebrations, hopes, and dreams that were shared created a deeper and more abiding vision of who I was and who we were as a family. Both of my great grandfathers fought in the Civil War; my mother's grandfather fought for the South and my dad's for the North. So my grandparents would share what they heard and what the aftermath of that war meant to people in the latter half of the nineteenth century. I learned that my maternal grandfather had been captured near a town where I was currently living. He escaped to share his story later; future generations (I and all of the others in the room) were beneficiaries of his escape. This reality was very profound to me as a child. Yes, we kept hearing the same stories over and over again, but as time went by I could see why they were important. Life was difficult for all of us, and the stories became beacons of hope and resilience that kept us going as we descended those mountaintops of meeting into the valleys of our living.

It also became a vision of what the rhythm of Eucharist is all about for me. As a family we came from the valleys of human existence and intentionally gathered as a community. In that community we shared stories, words, and actions of reassurance. We partook of food, conversation, and remembrance that made all of those sources of nourishment more than their initial presentation. We said prayers asking for God's blessing on our lives. We were then dismissed to carry this new life into the world yet again.

In this first week of Advent I am choosing to remember those stories. As I do I am well aware that others may not have such a story or perhaps have stories that are almost too horrific to want to remember, or have not felt that connection with their heritage. This first week of Advent is a good time to remember that it is never too late to dig wells of future memories for others. By being a resource, listener, and "valuer" of others, we can help create a "new memory" that can serve as a future memory for others.

This is one reason why it is most crucial not to give up on others. We may not be able to make a difference on an ongoing basis, but knowing that we have not given up on others or ourselves can create the possibility of a new start. This is not easy to do and it takes much prayer, perseverance, hard work, and forgiving, but it can be the start that makes all the difference in our lives and in the lives of others.

The stories we remember may involve a whole myriad of human experience. We can remember them in ways that help us move forward, often with the assistance of others; giving them voice helps us to come to terms with them. Our only option doesn't need to be stuck by them or defined by them. We can begin to break through to new insights, actions, relationships, and hopes. The persistent love of God is part of our history, and in this season of Advent it is available to us to make happen again.

Reflect

1. What are the most significant stories for you?
2. How have these stories affected your life and given definition to your identity and values?
3. What new stories are you yearning to create?

Now What?

This is perhaps life's most persistent question. It is on the precipice of the past and future as it becomes known to us in our verbal exclamation as well as non-verbal, moving to a new experience. Perhaps we have been to a sacred place or experienced an encounter that filled our spirits, or come through a day that has been significant, challenging, and full. We may wonder at that moment: Now what? At the end of a worship service, we may hear these words, "Let us go forth," or "Go in peace," or "Let us bless the Lord." At that moment in time, whether we verbalize it or not, we are entering the space called: Now what?

Life is certainty and mystery, breathing and exhaling, giving and taking, fearful and expectant, despairing and hopeful, joyful and sad, hurtful and healing, measured and unpredictable, full and empty, engaged and lonely—encompassing the whole range of feelings and experiences. When I was growing up, we had an expression when we encounter life at its depth—we called it "real," for that is what it was. We may feel similarly today, and in that feeling we may ask: What next?

As we look through our religious tradition, we will encounter myriads of times when people have encountered the Holy Other and asked: What now? For life at its depth and breadth most often calls for a response. It is at this point that other discriminating factors set in—our fears can take over, our self-doubts can hold sway, or our yearning for a new expression of life propels us either to consider a new response or pulls us back into our default positions that have helped inform who we are. Where is there an opportunity to look at who we are, what we yearn for, and who we wish to be? In any event it has the opportunity to create new possibilities for us.

Many years ago I was working on a denominational staff and enjoyed creating new possibilities for our life and work together. A very helpful colleague, Bishop Franklin D. Turner, would often offer these words, "What is the 'so that . . .' you are wishing to achieve or impact?" I found that if I kept asking the "so that" question, it would help me respond to the "now what" question. In other words, where is my response leading me, what is it that I wish to do and accomplish, and how do I propose getting there? The "now what" question was most helpfully engaged when I also answered the "so that" question. In doing so it would usually take me several rounds of questioning before I came to my next way station of work. Of course, life is not so easily engaged in this way, as the next moment often brings twists and turns and new possibilities that then bring new questions. How might we engage this journey without being too dizzy in trying to sort it all out? This brings us to fully living in the present moment.

The present moment, however fleeting, can bring us to a centered space of incorporation. This present moment can be described in millisecond terms, but it can become a space that helps us incorporate the past with our anticipation of the future. Through deep breathing, prayer, quiet reflection, deep silence, listening to the still small voice speaking to us, we can be still enough to let our spirits, emotions, feelings, and thoughts catch up to us. That space can create a new mosaic of life within us—in that space is often born anew the questions "what now" and "so that . . . ."

This can be difficult to do. Today the gift of Advent presence is awaiting us. The entrance to its foyer is not something we are rushing to do, but rather an opening for our hearts to experience what might be dwelling within us or beckoning us from in not so obvious ways. What is that life that is within us that wants to be expressed through us?

Years ago my dad and I were on a bus to the city. I saw many church steeples passing by as we traversed a road filled with little communities. I asked my dad, "How is it that we have so many churches and we cannot get along any better?" He responded, "That is a very good question." I waited for something more from him, but what he shared was what he shared. He knew I would need to wrestle with this question throughout my life. The various times when I wanted to respond to the "now what" or "so that" of my activity in life are times when I sought to live into the broader question: Why (and how) can we get along better?

In the myriad activities of our life (and this Advent), how can we find moments to just "be" so that in our being we might discover something new within and around us that just might make all the difference to us and to the world?

Reflect

1. What are those most significant experiences that have helped shape your life? Who has been there? Is there a single moment that stands out? Or is there a single person who stands out for you?
2. What is the "now what" or the "so that . . ." you wish for in your life?
3. What is waiting for you?

Where Is This Leading Me?

As we journey in life, we often ask the question: Where is this leading me? The "this" in the question can come in many forms. It may be a new relationship, a calling, an encounter that begs a response, a realization about health or status of life, or a myriad other things. We may want to back off and not be led, or we may be quizzical and wonder what might happen next. Life is full of voices and people who may want to lead us somewhere. This is where discernment comes in. Discernment is the capacity to see and understand something when the path may not be so readily apparent. It is looking at a path or decision from many angles, gathering our sources of authority, and listening to our "gut." Because the direction may not be so readily apparent, it usually takes some time. However, there are times when discernment needs to be swift and certain.

While in seminary I worked with people living on the streets of New York City, helping with a pastoral care desk at a local church. People (mostly men) would come into our place of hospitality with a number of different issues. One day as I was leaving I witnessed a man beating a child with a broken-off broom handle. I immediately confronted him, pinned him with my arms and body, and took the stick away from him. The child (unknown) ran away. I called out for help. Finally a police car arrived and arrested the man. They drove him away. I never heard anything more about it and often wonder what happened to him and to the child. Discernment needed to be swift and decisive, but the outcome in this case was somewhat unclear. Discernment leads to an action, which is both within our means and beyond our capacity to affect ultimately. Life is complex.

In other times, discernment took place over periods of time. I would meet people who may have given a first impression that was not pleasant, but I would ask myself if that was who that person really was. It took a period of time to begin to understand and even appreciate who they were, even then realizing I only knew a fraction of the person and his or her story. We often feel pressured to make a decision quickly, and the voices coming to us encourage us to do just that. As one of my sons often says, "It is what it is." In all of this we may ask the question: Who or what is leading me?

The question "Who is leading me?" is a question for the ages. It is asked throughout our religious traditions. The disciples had to come to terms with the answer to that question. Monks and sisters in monastic communities asked that question. We struggle with that question when we come up against making a moral decision or taking a certain action. In contemporary times, Martin Luther King, Jr. asked that question and found his answer at the mountaintop of his spiritual journey. How we answer that question leads to taking the actions we choose to take.

In the Episcopal Church we often speak of three sources of authority: scripture, tradition, and reason. We are informed and led by a conversation within and between these sources as we seek to make important decisions. Most recently people had added another dimension, which might be seen by itself or added to our understanding of reason. It is the wisdom that comes from a community of faith that is wrestling with a question.

Behind this question of "who is leading me" comes another question: What is the basis upon which I live my life? It is being concerned not only with questions about who is leading me or even where I might be going, but also "who am I" as I encounter this question. What has brought me to this place of understanding? This can be the gift of Advent. It is a time to look at our past and what has brought us to this moment. It is relishing in the fact that God's love knows no bounds and seeks to be incarnated not only in the birth of God's Son but also within us. Our actions and reactions are also to be incarnated within human life. What we do, how we see ourselves and others, and how we respond to human need and the needs of creation matter—to God and to us all.

What is that gift that we are searching to give? What does that gift have to do with our core values of who we are and who is the other? We may be led to an expression of a larger gift that we yearn to give. A gift contemplated for another person is one way we honor that person. It does not have to be something we buy but rather something we are committed to give. Perhaps the greatest gift we can give to another is the peace of God. We wish one another peace because the One who leads us is about peace, love, forgiveness, reconciliation, and healing. Our physical gift can be but one expression of our commitment to the other. So the size or expense of the gift is not nearly as important as our commitment and love behind the gift.

Gifts can come to us in abundance as we discern the holiness of lives faithfully lived, courage in the face of struggle, commitment to a heritage that gives life meaning and purpose, hope in the midst of discouragement, promise in the face of death, perseverance in the throes of incalculable odds, and in a whole host of other ways. These persons and their lives can lead us if we would pause long enough to follow. As I pause in writing these words, I can remember the faces, encounters, and gifts from those in my past and present.

Reflect

1. Who is leading you?
2. What is the basis upon which you live your life?
3. What gifts have others given you?

Discovery

Who Are We?

Look Around,
Look Behind

For a photographer, mid-day can be a particular challenge. The shadows are not quite right, the light may even be a little too bright, and everything can seem a little too washed out. Yet it is in the mid-day when life at its fullness is lived out. While working in New York City it was easy for me to jump and follow the crowd wherever it was going. I had a destination and loved to walk there without ever stopping—timing my walk so that I would zigzag across the City without being stopped by traffic. I would do this walk usually looking ahead or looking down with recognition of those persons around me. One day I started looking for random acts of kindness. Yes, on the streets of New York City, random acts of kindness are manifold. My discovery of a laundromat called *That Missing Sock* may have triggered my new attitude of looking around and behind me.

The name of the laundromat intrigued me. Surely, I thought, this is one of the primal questions we may take with us to the pearly gates: How come we only get three-and-a-half pairs back when we put four pairs of socks in the dryer? One day I decided to take my laundry to *That Missing Sock* and because I did, my life was changed. On that fateful day a woman welcomed me generously as I entered the laundromat. She asked if I needed help doing my laundry. I responded, "I generally can use some help in everything I do." She responded, "Use washer 1, 4, and 5. Avoid the rest." Then she added, "Dryers 1, 3, and 5 are fabulous. Avoid the rest." I had never been welcomed with such directness to a laundromat or any place else for that matter. She then wondered if I could use some help with the soap and the softener. "For sure," I responded. Together we sat and watched my clothes begin to be washed. I thought she must be the owner or manager but discovered she was just there doing her wash, too. We talked some more and she shared her visions of people around the world washing their clothes in rivers and our conversation turned to talk about baptism in the rivers as a kind of washing. She had no idea I was a priest. Intrigued by her, I asked if she had had breakfast, and if not, might we grab something to eat at which she directed me to her favorite deli. For the next couple of hours we watched our clothes wash and dry as we enjoyed breakfast with one another. During these hours I experienced several people entering the laundromat, sharing their personal stories of angst and celebration with her, as well as asking for her advice. In a special way she was the priest-rabbi-shaman of this place. We have been friends ever since.

Some time later, in speaking with Lyndon Harris, former vicar of St. Paul's Chapel near Ground Zero, I shared this story, as well as many other happenstance conversations I often find myself engaged in. He spoke of "third meaning making places" where people exchange deep questions of life, seek meaning in the midst of chaos, and yearn for companionship and hope along the way. This was indeed true at St. Paul's following the tragedy of 9/11 and was true in *The Missing Sock*. Where might those places be for you?

As I started looking for random acts of kindness in the City, I started seeing them in a way I had never seen before. I wonder, who else around us is very special? How will we know? As we enter more deeply into the Advent season in the mid-day and at other times, we might just discover more fully what life at its breadth and depth is all about—looking around us and behind us.

Reflect

1. What and who are you looking for today?
2. Who is in your midst?
3. What more might you discover?

Discovering Our Identity

One of the realizations we have in life is that our identity is not only complex, but changes throughout life. "Who am I?" has been answered in different ways in the contexts of my life.

There are many ways I might share my identity including: child of God, child of Melford and Hilda Holland, brother to Nancy, born and bred in West Virginia, a man, a husband, a father, grandfather, friend, companion, inquirer, photographer, storyteller, priest, consultant, coach, musician, dancer, person of prayer, appreciator of life, reflector of life experiences, person of hope, lover of the created order, citizen of the United States, fellow journeyer with the world . . . well the list could go on and on. What would that list be for you?

We are who we are and are also defined by others, discovering who we are in relationship with others. Others may make a similar list of who they perceive we are. What might others in your life say about you?

As we live into the Advent season, I encourage you to reflect on your past, wonder about your future, all the while seeking to live in the present moment (which becomes past for us even as we speak). Where does our exploration of our past take us as we think about our emerging identity?

When we journey into our past we can readily see that our identity has taken on new descriptions and complexities. There may be things about ourselves that we have put on the shelf that we would like to take off the shelf and engage. For me, it is playing the piano. I began playing the piano when I was three years old, taking lessons and progressing steadily until about the fourth grade. At that point I was not interested in practicing the piano, but more interested in spending time with my friends and playing sports. So I quit taking lessons. As I reflect back on that decision, I now regret it. I could have picked it up over the years again and again but did not. So I am now one who plays the piano by ear. A decision awaits me: Am I going to pick it up again at my age or not? Other interests may come to mind for you. What is on your shelf in life? Do you want to pick it up again?

We know from a variety of sources that identity development begins at a very young age. Many people have grown up feeling as though they are of little worth. Their identity might be expressed more in terms of negative feelings than positive ones. We all have negative and life-draining experiences throughout our lifetimes, but some of us have more than our fair share. When we think of inviting people to examine their past, it can be very tricky and risky. At any point in our journey we can do something positive: treat the other with self-respect, recognize their value and importance in life, and be willing to stand with them in their lives.

For many of us it is not just about discovering our identity but rediscovering that part of our identity that has become hidden from us. For others the question may not materialize as life in all of its complications is crashing down with such ferocity that there seems to be no time for such reflections. Yet we know that this has been, and continues to be, a seminal question for humanity. Perhaps we saw our identity much more interconnected with our broader community than we do now. The fractious way in which we live much of our life has us connected with the global village and nearby communities while at the same time urging us to develop our individuality. We may feel torn between these powerful voices in our midst. Both our individual and communal identities are important. In the United States, these identities complement and compete against one another in many significant ways, especially in the pressures surrounding Advent.

We discover our identities in a myriad of ways. One of those ways is in the wilderness, where most all of us have been at one or more times in our life. The wilderness can be a place of respite, renewal, and rebirth, but at the same time it can be a place of loneliness, hopelessness, fear, and disorientation.

Wilderness can compel us to enter or push us away with a sense of foreboding. It can be a place, a situation in life, a broken relationship, a death of a loved one, work that is unsatisfying, bereavement that absorbs our life spirit, a place where we come to terms with who we are and yearn to be, and a place of transformation.

Jesus often went into the wilderness to pray, reflect, be renewed, and to gain his center. John the Baptist found the wilderness conducive to his preaching repentance and baptizing. Wilderness can be an emotional, physical, or spiritual space in the created order. Wilderness is most helpfully negotiated when we have a companion along the way, but it can often be experienced alone. However difficult it may feel to be in the wilderness, it is also the cauldron of new life and possibilities, new hopes and dreams, new birth. It is a needed place for most of us to come to terms with our histories and our spirituality.

In this second week of Advent we may be experiencing a sense of being in the wilderness. In this season of life we may experience life as increasingly complex with voices from our tradition, culture, our personally held deep values clashing with our human experience—all of which can be confusing. Messages of consumerism, preparations, and rushing around can overwhelm us—all the more reason to venture into the waters that we may call wilderness, knowing that God meets us in the wilderness, troubling the waters with the Spirit.

Advent is a gift from the past, created to help us prepare for the birth of Christ. It is a period of reflection, taking stock in order to embrace most fully the meaning of that birth in our lives. As such it is embraced by others who share this perspective and is virtually unknown by others in our midst. As this broader community is the community in which we live, to embrace the journey of Advent takes some intentionality and purposefulness. Pressures come in ways that urge us to rush by Advent or to avoid it altogether. We live in the now but are informed by the past. What is it that we have learned about ourselves by looking at our past? How are those learnings shaping our journey and identity in the present and giving perspective on where we might be going? How do we come to terms with the pressures and opportunities of preparation for Christmas gift giving and receiving as well as hosting, but in ways that help us engage the deeper contemplation of wondering why God shared God's Son. How does God's gift affect the world and what difference might that make to our identity?

The question of "Who am I now?" is still a question for us in this second week of Advent. We ask it again because it is a life question—a question that journeys with us through a lifetime.

I took many bus trips with my family when I was a young boy. I remember the sights and smells within the bus, the towns that were new to my memory as we drove through the hollows of our land, and the contours of the communities. Within those trips I remember asking many questions such as: What do the people do in these communities? Where are we going? Are we getting close? And there are many more. I would find some answers for myself, my parents and sister would answer others, and there were still others greeted by the response: "That is a good question." Yes, there are some questions that cannot be readily answered and some that we need to live into. The answers may come in time and then new questions will emerge. This seems to be the rhythm of life, as we know it. Such is the case with our identity. We know the "we" we are for now, but understand that who we are will emerge in new ways as we live life.

In this second week of Advent how are you exploring yet again your identity? Where is that exploration taking you? Advent is the season that describes most fully our life journey as it seeks to remind us of our past and to anticipate our future, while grounding us in the present moments of our life quest. It is the beginning of a new church year and the beginning again of our journey to reflect on the meaning of life and the meaning of our lives.

Reflect

1. How might you find some ways to keep asking these life questions, including the meaning of your identity now?
2. Who am I? Who are we? Whose are we? Who is the "we" we yearn to be? What are those life questions for you?
3. Where is and what is the "there" when we might say: Are we there yet?

People of the Gathering

We are the people of the gathering. We come to our gatherings out of the complicated context of our living. As we gather we bring our contexts with us, as the gathering is also part of our context. But why do we gather? Is it to gain some perspective, nourishment, solace, meaning, or perhaps all of that and more?

Over the history of time, people have gathered for myriads of reasons. Some of our time is solitary and most of us need some solitary, alone time. Yet we seem to be drawn to gatherings, large and small, to have a deeper sense of who we are, where we have been, where we might be going, what we value, and what life is all about at a greater depth. Sometimes we gather and want to close the circle. At other times we create permeable circles of trust where others can easily enter the circle. Gatherings are for protection, relationship and trust building, and meaning making.

Advent is a time when we experience intentional and unintentional gatherings at perhaps their zenith in the year. As a young boy living in a small village in West Virginia, I experienced gatherings in many ways. In our village of four hundred people, I could easily walk or ride my bike to everyone's home. Gatherings were defined in part by our geography, whether it was across the road or a little to the west. The valley was sprinkled with small towns and villages built by the companies that had businesses in the valley. Each appeared to be self-contained, yet each did not provide the full services needed by the community. We needed to drive our cars, catch buses, or take long walks to access the services we needed. Each of the communities had their own identities, relationships, and sometime large family units. In Falls View I had a total of twenty-one first cousins, but I now have no relatives left in that village or any of the other villages along the valley. A nostalgic and somewhat lonely feeling.

Throughout the ages villages and other communities were organized to facilitate contact, to build businesses to support the livelihood and basic nourishment needs of their inhabitants, to provide protection from others who may be seen as unwelcomed visitors, and as a place, a habitation. Even in great cities like New York City, Philadelphia, or San Francisco, the importance of communities within the larger community are significant. It is hard to get one's mind and arms around a huge community but we can in smaller expressions of community. We gather in larger communities as we yearn for relationships with people with whom we can share life and vitality in small, more manageable doses.

Advent is a time when our communities well up around us and within us. It is a time of being surrounded by others, often finding us in a dance of activities, including the preparation for those gatherings. It is a time for being surprised as we may find new meaning in our internal and external journeys. It is also a time of loneliness and sadness as we remember loved ones who have died, hopes dashed by the realities of life, and peace becoming ever so elusive. Gatherings can be people, memories, hopes, and recognitions of sadness and joy. Gatherings can be life giving, renewing, struggling, tenuous, full of meanings, or vacant of joy. As human beings we are dependent on them to create and sustain our lives. It is the interaction and mutual dependency of change and structure that keeps our bodies alive and our communities vibrant and sustaining. As we journey through Advent, we can catch a glimpse of these realities in the rush that seems be building up around us and within us.

There were many times as a young boy when I sought to distance myself from my community to gain some silence and perspective of life. I would either take long walks, go into the woods, drive up the roads leading outside the valley, or even go into the closest city, Charleston, to gain some solitary space in a more crowded space where I was not known. Cities can be very lonely spaces while also being places of intentional alone time. I always felt drawn to cities; I would read about them and make maps incorporating them as I dreamed about travel. My earlier dreams ultimately came true as my work as an adult included much travel to cities near and far. But I especially recall the small gatherings of family and friends, classmates, fraternity brothers, and sports buddies as we reflected on life as we enjoyed other interactions. I miss seeing them but they are not gone from my memory.

Sometimes we are reluctant to connect with communities and other gatherings outside our personal orbit because we may not feel welcomed or of value to engage others in this way. As I have worked and encountered people who lived on the streets, I would ask them their name; I also offered mine. I never had an instance when someone did not share his or her name. There is something powerful in a name and to be recognized by name. It positions us into a relationship, into a small or larger community. It recognizes us as a person of worth, a person with a unique history.

Through social media, Episcopal bishop Steven Charleston welcomes people to share in an online community gathering to offer prayers. It is a wonderful invitation and a reminder that gatherings can now occur anywhere at anytime. These gatherings (when well intentioned and healthy) can be ways to get connected, stay connected, and reconnect with family and friends. It may not be as real or salutatory as face-to-face, but it can be rich and meaningful—and it is what we have available to help us stay in touch. As Advent means "coming," we have yet to see what is coming in information technology, but are beginning to see glimpses of the future of new ways of being community over the horizon.

Reflect

1. What is in your name? Where does your name take you in your reflection about your past and other gatherings that have gone on before in your life and history?
2. In your gatherings with others, what has been most significant for you?
3. What is it that you yearn for as you contemplate new gatherings?

People of the Table

We are a people of the context, a people of the gathering, and a people of the table. What is the table? How important might a table be to us in our physical, emotional, relational, and spiritual journeys?

Tables can come in many shapes and sizes, purposes and meanings. They are places where nourishment of food, drink, and conversation are consumed, places of preparation for work to be accomplished, places to lay out our plans, and places of opportunities to share with others.

One of the most important tables in my home is my dining room table. It seats eight people and offers a genial space and place for entertaining family and friends. It is sufficient in size to have place settings for each person along with other space in the middle for candles and anything else we might want to put in close reach. But it is special to me because it was a meeting ground for my family when I was very young, and has been a place of conversation and reconnection for me with family and friends over the years, representing the gatherings of so many over the years. As I look at the table, I am drawn to days gone by as well as anticipating new ones coming my way.

Tables can be places where we are especially open to a vision of life that informs us about the meaning of life itself. Tables can be holy tables like in a worship space, dining tables, work tables, tables of conversation and work together, or even mountain tops or mesas where the vistas of life around us and within us shine in a new way. As we engage in gatherings that lead us to new meaning and reflection, we can find ourselves at a table where larger visions might occur. Tables can also be sidewalks, train platforms, or any place where a circle of conversation or intentional in-depth sharing takes place. Tables can be both physical and virtual as they serve as settings for conversations of meaning making.

Another platform (table) where I shared conversation and prayers over the years was on a street corner with one who camped out at that location. When hearing I was leaving the City, he said, "It will be okay because God closes the distance between us." On that space we were elevated to other spaces of our imaginations and sharing, offered up people in our prayers, and shared more than just a few laughs. And on that space we both caught a vision again of God's love and presence, which knows no bounds. It is a table that will be forever etched in my memory.

In Advent it can be difficult to find such tables; in the rush for buying presents or window-shopping (does anyone do this any more?), tables can be taken. We may be seated alone at a table, with an empty chair that seems to beckon someone else to join us, but they don't. How many tables do we see that could seat three or four people but only has one? What prevents us from asking if we could sit there, too? We may not want to be intrusive and the person at the table may want that private space, but it may just be an opportunity to explore shared space grown out of private space.

In the hot summer months my mother and I would wait for my dad to come home from the metallurgical plant. He arrived home within a ten-minute window—between 5:10 and 5:20—like clockwork. Together we would go up on the mountain to Hawks Nest for a picnic supper. On the mountain it was cooler; being nestled into trees and greenery felt good at the end of a hot day. We would wind our way there—about a thirty-minute drive. After our meal at one of the picnic tables we would visit the overlook over the New River Gorge and then take an extended drive for the next hour or more. While we were driving we talked. Yes, we ate at picnic tables at the park, but we also had another table within the car that gathered us around for conversation and exploration. It was in those moments when I realized the value of sharing space on the mountaintops of our living. Those trips made all the difference to me in my life. It was years before Dr. Martin Luther

King, Jr. uttered those words in Memphis, but I heard them echoing from within me: I have been to the mountaintop and I am no longer afraid.

Being at table can be a place of resolution, vision making, building community and relationships, dreaming new dreams, singing new songs, and finding nourishment for our well-worn bodies and spirits. It can also be lonely, sad, and depleting. What might we do to create tables within us and before us that can strengthen our resolve, build our sense of self-esteem, offer possibilities of hearing some new words and wisdom and finding a new meaning for ourselves in life?

During Advent we build upon tables long gone before where people gathered at Seder meals, in places of worship, on dusty roads of travel, in places of bereavement and sorrow, on other hillsides, valleys, or seashores. All seeking to make sense of life, where God might be in the world and in their lives, and how they may have the courage to proceed with hope. It is my hope that you might find that table in your life and that in finding it, your life will be filled with new promise and purpose.

Reflect

1. What does being at table mean for you? Who is there with you?
2. What vision, work, or meaning-making experience occurs at the tables at which you sit? How might you learn about your vocation or mission in life by being at table?

3. Where might be the tables in your life where the depth of life's experiences can be shared? What are those spaces for you and what space or table do you wish to be in your future?

People of the Dismissal

The word "dismissal" has much complexity depending on the contexts of its use. From my youth I can remember the excitement of being freed from the classroom to go play or go home. Dismissal felt like freedom. Dismissal can also feel like being discounted, not valued, or not heard. We use statements in the Episcopal Church's liturgies to note the end of the service: "Let us go forth in the name of Christ" or "Go in peace to love and serve the Lord." Even in those worship experiences it means so much more for we are a "people of the dismissal."

As a people of the dismissal we know that our journey does not end with the gathering or even at the tables of vision making. Our journeys take us back into the varied contexts of our living where life is shared and engaged at its depth. It is a declaration that the journey is not just about us individually or even as a small group of people, but also with all the diversity of perspectives that await us. Peter, James, and John understood this as Peter's wish to build three booths on the mountaintop of Christ's transfiguration (Matthew 17:1–13) was overridden by the walk that was to follow—that journey into the weeds of human despair would ultimately end in Jerusalem, and later spread to Galilee and to the whole world.

Each of our major religious traditions has a dismissal within them. Each has a component of how to treat others and value their worth. Advent encourages us to engage in introspection, to take stock of who we are, how we are doing, and how we wish to be born in ourselves yet again; we are also reminded that the journey is not just for us or about us. It is also about sharing life with others. It is about being in the world, taking God's message to others. We can sense this as we search for gifts for others, but it is a reminder that giving gifts to others is so much more than physical presents, as wonderful as they might be. The gifts of peace, love, kindness, healing, forgiveness, challenge, intellectual pursuit, and a whole number of other gifts come to mind.

Sometimes in our searching for a gift we find other gifts beyond our imagining. We sometimes dismiss what is close at hand, something that is right in front of us that we do not notice. On a cold snowy day a year ago I was searching for a gift for a colleague. I looked in many stores, including a large mall some distance away, maneuvering over icy roads that taxed my driving ability. Still, no present. Returning to a store close to my home, I finally found the right gift and got in line at the register. Suddenly I heard a familiar voice of an old friend whom I had not seen for over thirty years. I wondered if it was he; how could it be him as he lives in Indonesia? I looked back and it was true. I approached him with, "I think I know you." And he exclaimed, "Bud Holland, what are you doing here?" We embraced. His accompanying daughter cried and so did we. It was a gift I was not expecting, but one that I will never forget.

What does it mean for us to be a dismissed people? That is very different from being a people who dismisses other people. It means, in part, that we identify with the people with whom we serve. All of us have experienced being dismissed, disregarded, or disrespected. All have experienced the feeling that our ideas have been dismissed without consideration or they themselves have been let go without cause. As a people of the dismissal, we are also called to leave our rooms filled with fear in order to enter other rooms filled with fear. We know what it is to be afraid and we can be determined to not let that memory keep us from others who may feel the same. This was the urging that Jesus expressed to the disciples as they crowded into a room filled with fear (John 20:19–23). He urged them to leave that room and bring good news to others so huddled. Love and good news are made manifest when they are shared.

Sometimes we may want to huddle in a small room as life is swirling around us. We may want to hunker down with a good book, some solitary time, a drink of choice, and not more than one companion at a time. That is understandable and often good for the soul. We too need a retreat! Yet we know that it is not the end or summation of our journey. Advent draws us back in history and forward to what might lie next, all the while inviting us to be present to our present moments. It is a tall order, but one which most clearly reflects life's journey. Why do I like Advent? It most fully offers me a window of life that mimics the rest of my life. The present moment is what I have. The past moments are what I have in my present memory. The future moments are what I have in my present imagination. Yes, Advent presence: kissed by the past, beckoned by the future, dismissed as people of God's love.

So what do we make of all this in our present moments? We are asked to gather, to connect with one another at table, and to be dismissed to join with others in the varied contexts of our living. The meanings and connotations of all those steps coming to us at once can feel overwhelming. So may we, in our dismissal, be mindful of the overwhelming nature of life's quests and circumstances, and in our calling to be a dismissed people to be about God's work with courage and with God's help.

Reflect

1. What is it like to be dismissed people?
2. What gives you a sense that you may be a bearer of good news, hope, and promise? What do you need to make this work?
3. How should we proceed (to be a dismissed people)? How will we know we are proceeding?

Reengaging Contexts

One of the most exhilarating yet humbling journeys we might take is to go to a high school reunion. I have been to several over the years. At a fortieth-year reunion we gathered for pictures on an outdoor deck of the meeting place—just next to the Kanawha River in West Virginia. Two of the members of our class looked like they had just gotten off the bus from school. They looked so young and robust. When I received a copy of the group photo, it seemed like all the rest of us were leaning away from them. There they were, on one side of the picture with the rest of us on the other. Does this reflect how reticent we might be to reenter a context? For we don't know what we will find there. Perhaps even our old selves will be in the new picture.

Reunions have interesting conversations of shared stories and memories: missed tackles on the football field, teachers who were dear to our memory and those who were not, the car crashes we were involved in, and a whole host of other remembered events. All of that is wonderful and predictable. But what about people's lives now? What have our lives been about since high school and what is it that we want to do now? We don't allow enough time to get to those questions. We can be stuck in the past and look at the other as those they once were: the eighteen-year-old friend. They are now much older, like us, and have so much more to tell about themselves.

One of the most difficult places we can be in life is to prejudge people based on past data. In John 1:46 we read how Jesus was prejudged by just being the son of Joseph and Mary, having come from Nazareth. In my childhood we prejudged people who lived down the valley, up the hollows, any other place that was different from the narrow slice of geography where we lived. We didn't like some others because they didn't like us—we were rivals on the football fields and basketball courts of our living. Yet as we grow older, how might we entertain letting go of that kind of bigotry and prejudice?

One of the powerful forces in our lives is that of default. It is that position to which we return, as it defines for us a point in time where we feel more secure about who we are and the world around us. It matters less if the default is working well for us, but it does matter a lot if we remain stuck there. A default position held in high school should certainly be reexamined as we age. Default can be a place of comfort, recognized space, and safety, but it can also be a place where we remain at our peril. Being open to identify, reacquaint, and readjust ourselves from default positions that don't serve us or anyone else well is a worthy journey for us all. A worthy example is Peter, who after the resurrection went back to fishing even though he did not seem to be a great fisherman. This is what he knew to do. He was pursued by the post-resurrection Jesus and urged to follow a different path. It is hard to be present with the living God and new good news when go back to where we were before.

Being a photographer I have become more sensitive to events, people, light, shadows, connections of colors, hues, and occasional sightings that I might have missed before. So in the hustle and bustle of everyday life, I try to be more intentional about recognizing random acts of kindness. Yes, I find them everywhere. Many seem to be without words. People are listening to one another, assisting one another to negotiate the sidewalks and street corners, and laughing with one another about who knows what. I am learning to change my default position from people who are primarily interested in getting from point A to point B, to people who are also interested in caring for each other along the way. Not everyone is like this, but I have discovered many more than I originally imagined. Walking thirty blocks to work in a city while taking different routes each time helped me get to work with my spirits uplifted. Such is the possibility of changing our default positions, even if only just a little bit. I was reengaging the contexts of my living.

Reengaging the contexts of our living means that we are bringing our full, newly evolving selves with us.

Reflect

1. What is that full self that you want to express during this Advent?
2. How are you seeking to reengage your contexts of living?
3. What are you observing? What difference does your observation bring?

Accomplishments and Gifts

Many of us have accomplishments and gifts that are unknown to us. At the conclusion of workshops we are often asked to identify the gifts of those in the group, sharing them with each individual. Sometimes those gifts were a surprise to the receiver; occasionally others see them differently. How and why does this often happen? Perhaps we are so focused on the work to be done that we don't take the time to identify the collection of gifts and talents that made it possible. Additionally, some of us are programmed to not think highly of ourselves so we don't readily see our contribution for the gift it is. Of course, some people have overinflated notions of their gifts and accomplishments, but I would surmise that most of us have an under-appreciation of them.

The energy to move forward in creative ways is fueled by our strengths, achievements, gifts, and talents. We need to solve some problems along the way but when we use our best gifts, do what we enjoy doing, work in an environment where we share similar core values, we have the greatest potential to do our best work. In the midst of this Advent, let us pause to think about ourselves in terms of accomplishments and gifts. We might need someone or a number of others to help us with this one.

As we think more fully about our accomplishments and gifts, we have the opportunity to assist others to do the same. There is no better way to start than at the beginning of life and in the early years of maturation. Setting a new environment of learning, helpful encouragement, and reinforcing the value of young children in our midst is crucial to them throughout their lifetimes. While serving in a church in the inner city, I asked one of the church school teachers what curriculum was being used. She said they welcomed young people into the circle, assured them of God's love, and said they were valued and treasured. She then spoke about how they offered them breakfast, followed by a game or other activity along with a lesson from the Bible or another aspect of our religious tradition. Throughout the time together the children were in a safe, hospitable space. The children were told in many ways they were loved by God, were treasured, and were sent forth with hopes to see them again soon. The basic underpinning of being assured we are people of worth in God's sight and in ours is so crucial to building a learning community.

However, life can be difficult, complex, and full of blunders created by us all. To wind our way through the maze of these situations, we need the development of coping skills, the capacity to persevere and be resilient, the determination to begin again, and the support of others along the way. All of this is hard work and is not easy. To develop the capacity to keep on keeping on is a journey of youth, middle age, and older adulthood. The forces within our lives to chip away at that capacity are legion. So is our collective capacity to be present for others. Being aware of these pushes and pulls, especially during this busy time of year, can be a gift to others as well as ourselves.

Giving up can also be a gift. We let go of our fears, our need for control, and the insatiable need for accumulation in order to make space in our lives for new life and possibilities. One of the most important questions we have in life is: What are we open to letting go? It is the journey we make in our spiritual lives that opens us up to hear the still, small voice of God, the voices crying out within us to find expression in our living, or the worry that keeps us from embracing life at its full. Letting go of relationships that are demeaning, degrading, or void of healthy interaction can be life giving. Letting go of the assumptions that we have all the right answers so that we cannot listen to others can be freeing. Letting go of those things that impede a deeper human relationship with others is essential for our growth and place in a broader community of fellow sojourners. So letting go is important. Also important is the not letting go of love, concern, valuing of others and ourselves, and hope (whenever possible). We all need some retreat time, some wilderness time, some time to just be as we are also called to be a part of a larger human family. To take heart and take courage to face the often-perilous times also involves letting go and taking on.

We are close to the midway point in this Advent journey. Anticipate some pause in our penitential reflections and anticipate a recognition that tomorrow will be a day when we focus on joy and celebration. In many churches the blue or purple candles on the Advent wreath give way in this time to the pink candle highlighting this transition. Every Sunday in the Christian tradition is a Sunday of celebration, but this upcoming Sunday especially reminds us of the importance of celebrating the course of our living, giving thanks for all that has been, and hoping beyond hope that we might be able to say "yes" to all that follows—"yes" to embracing life and to let life embrace us with all of its potential learning and possibilities.

One of the gifts of aging for me is realizing that I cannot do everything that I used to be able to do, but that frees me up to do something new and to try to do it the best I can. It is the gift of letting go, holding on, and giving my life to something and someone(s) in ways that matter. May it be so for you.

Reflect

1. Why is it important that we recognize our gifts and accomplishments?
2. What is important for you to let go of in order to experience life in its fullness?
3. What is it that you yearn to accomplish and how might you see yourself doing just that? What help and support do you need to do it?

Commitment

Whose Are We Now?

Celebrating Anyway

As we enter the third week of Advent, it is a time for taking stock and examining how we might be living our life that is not in sync with the way we believe our life should be lived. Depending on your church's tradition, the colors for Advent could be purple to emphasize penitence or blue, the color of anticipation of what is to come (often seen as the color of Mary). The third candle on the Advent wreath is often a soft pink, which is a reminder of the importance of celebration in the midst of our perspective of how imperfectly we may be living our lives. As such it is called *Gaudete* Sunday, Rose Sunday, which serves as this vivid reminder of the importance of celebration and rejoicing in our lives.

In the midst of our living we may come to a church for the celebration of Holy Eucharist. Eucharist (also known as Holy Communion, Last Supper, Mass) means thanksgiving. As such it becomes a celebration for us, no matter what time of year it is or what frame of mind we may be in.

This Sunday often falls on a date closest to my first-born son's birthday. I vividly remember when he was born. At our local hospital I was with Annie, my wife, as she experienced a long labor. Entering the hospital on Saturday morning proved a challenge as I was scheduled to preach the next day. It would not be a typical Sunday, as it was my last Sunday as a deacon and I was to be ordained priest three days later. While Annie labored, I worked on a sermon (not something I would recommend to any parent-to-be). Late Saturday evening I finally called the rector of the church where I was serving; I would not be able to preach the next day. He was very kind and understanding. Our son was born at one o'clock on Sunday afternoon and what a glorious celebration that was, especially for Annie. Three days later I was ordained priest.

As a young deacon and priest, I was given the responsibility of shepherding a newly organized congregation just completing their worship space. I was in charge of organizing the ordination service (which included ordaining ten deacons), as I was serving in a church closest to the ordination site. The service concluded, and as we began singing "Praise to the Lord the Almighty" for the recessional hymn, the bishop came racing off the altar and said to me, "Don't you know that we always sing 'Come Labor On' at all ordinations?" "No," I said.

"I did not know that. But, Bishop, you approved the service." His finger stopped in mid-air as he said, "I guess I need to look more carefully next time." For sure the words "Come Labor On" were not lost on me. However, I believe I chose the other hymn because this was a time of giving praise to God.

This church was so new that when we had our dedication service we realized we did not have offering plates. I shared with the bishop just before he made the offertory invitation that since we had no offering plates and people had given all of their offerings, time, and talent to construct this building that we would have no monetary offering this day. He responded, "We will have an offering today. On this first day of worship in this church, our first offering will go to the relief of widows and their families who have lost loved ones in the recent mining disaster. I want the ushers to retrieve their hats and we will pass the hat today!" So the first offering went to others in need. And so it is when we have our sight and our hearts set on mission and the struggles of people around us.

Having a celebration is not just about us. A birthday celebrates life itself. A worship experience propels us to the lonely, hungry person on the street or the family who feels famished without love, support, food, or hope. In a microcosm of experience we realize that we are indeed connected to the whole world.

I am often struck by the number of times we gather for a meal and conversation after a baptism, wedding, funeral, or other times involving important events in our lives. There is something special in the combination of food and conversation that provides nourishment that will help see us to another day as it feeds both our bodies and spirits. The ability of community to help us define for ourselves how we want to remember, to be reminded, and to be surprised by new beginnings in our life is the essence of being in relationship with another. For a moment in time we say we are in this together.

Giving birth takes many forms: new life, a new calling, a new community. Advent calls us to newness of life.

Reflect

1. In what ways might we give birth to new ideas, new life, or a different way of approaching our mission or ministry in life?
2. What do you want to celebrate today?
3. For what or whom do you grieve?

Whose Are We and Whose Am I?

O ne of the compelling questions in our time is: Whose are we? Allegiance, bonding, identification, relationship, servanthood, patriotism, and more are voices that seek to draw us into connection that defines, in part, who we are and leads us to whose we are. This question can be somewhat benign and offer a general description of belonging or it can be descriptive of a much more in-depth identification that carries with it a life path.

Growing up in West Virginia, we lived in "company" housing, got food from the "company" store, went to a "company" picnic at a park, played on a "company" little league baseball team, and enjoyed a regular news publication. Even though the company's identification was pervasive throughout the region, it was relatively thin for those of us who did not work for "the company." This phenomenon was duplicated up and down the valley as the company built housing and networks of activities to draw in employees and their families to make the company's work possible. One's life was much more defined by the culture of the valley and the identification with the industry of the plant. It was not easy to gain advancement in one's job. A sense of community developed that involved not only the plant, but also the communities themselves including school activities. I did not feel a special allegiance to the company but did feel an identity with it.

Identity is about one's self-understanding. It's about answering the question: Who am I? Related to this is: Whose am I? Who (or what) do I belong to? How many times do we respond to this question with answers such as a child of God or a follower of Jesus? One person who sets an example for me in living out the answers to such questions is Martin Luther King, Jr. Dr. King's life journey was inextricably connected to his answer to whose am I. His non-violent yet persistent, resilient approach to protest helped define a movement and led us to consider whom he was following. His life journey, however flawed like all of our life journeys, was a journey of a human being who had a choice in life in how he lived and chose to give his life so that others might have life in abundance. A loving, forgiving God, who also wanted justice and freedom for the people, consumed him. He lived his faith, was informed by his faith, and saw his identity as integrally connected by his faith, yet also respected others who had other faith journeys. He spoke for those who were poor, on the margins of life, and whose life journeys were truncated by prejudice and active discrimination.

Some important questions: Where is God in my life? What might God be calling me to be and to do? What might God be up to in the world and what does that mean to me? For what goals, dreams, companies, or institutions am I pouring out my life? For what am I spending or being spent? To what or to whom am I committed? With whom and with what group do I share my most sacred and private hope for my life and the lives of those whom I love? What are those sacred hopes, those most compelling goals and purposes of my life?

During Advent we recall others in our religious traditions who have wrestled with these big questions and more. This was a primal question in the Hebrew Scriptures from the time of Moses and extending through the times of the kings and prophets, and the wisdom literature. God makes a covenant with the people. The people try to keep the Covenant. The Covenant is broken and the price to pay for that brokenness becomes manifest. God brings about redemption and healing. The cycle of creation, sin, judgment, and redemption travels through the Hebrew Scriptures.

In the New Testament, the answer to "Who do you say that I am?" becomes a journey of identification and turning one's life over to God. It is more than a belief structure or the stating of a faith. It is a life transformation. The disciples, as well as we who follow this tradition, are encouraged not to go back to our default positions but to allow ourselves to be transformed into a new model of servanthood. This is seen in Holy Baptism and in the other rites of our sacred journeys in which we covenant with God to serve God's purposes in creation. We are to be raised to a new life of grace and in that unmerited love of God, to share the same with others.

From devoting our lives to the "company" to a transformation of our lives to follow the One who is in all our journeys, is a life journey for us all. Fundamentally, we are God's and life itself is a gift. How we live that out, if we choose to claim it, will occur in as many ways as there are sand particles on the shores of our lives. We are able to live out this reality in our own diverse ways; it is a freedom that honors our uniqueness while claiming our hearts.

Reflect

1. Whose are am I? Who (or what) do I belong to?
2. Where is God in my life? What might God be calling me to be and to do?
3. For what "companies" am I pouring out my life? For what am I spending or being spent?

Endings and Beginnings

Endings and beginnings are bookends to the present moment. They are all constantly on the move. So what to make of them? We understand our lives by looking backward but we live our lives by looking forward. Or do we? It assumes a level of health that helps us dance between the three (past, present, future). It also assumes a willingness to let go of some of our default positions that root ourselves too deeply in our past and any penchant we may have to dwell only in the future. Yet both the past and future are incredibly informative and important in shaping our present moments and emerging future. We cannot be in perfect balance all the time, but usually seek out actions to correct the imbalance.

Making adjustments becomes a way of life. Hence the expression: Been there, done that. Will be there again.

Some of this reality is seen in our dance with history that seems to repeat itself. I remember a friend who gave a biblical verse to someone making a life profession in a monastic order. The verse she gave was this: Be ye perfect as your Father in heaven is perfect. He blanched. She responded, "Of course we cannot be perfect. We are called to journey to wholeness. But what I wish for you is that you be perfectly yourself."

What is it that we can do in life? Perhaps we can live out our life as faithfully as we can, buoyed by deep values welling up within us, forgiving others and ourselves, and staying the course with others, some of whom need much support to move forward in good ways. We can have faith and courage that comes in part from God and others, still having faith that we will not be abandoned. Perhaps we can be that person who journeys with others, all the while valuing and treasuring them in these whirlwinds of life.

Many religious traditions offer the opportunity to share the peace of God with one another during worship. When we do we are never quite the same again and neither are they.

As we journey into the depth of Advent, we can realize that the heroic gifts in life often come in small gestures, an offer of an ear to hear, outstretched arms to embrace, or words of hope and presence to dispel overriding fear or despair. We all have something to offer—something that is totally unique. What seems like an ending for us or for another can be a new beginning. We can experience that in both giving and receiving.

Reflect

1. What does perfection mean to you?
2. What might you consider doing for another person or group?
3. What are we open to give and receive today?

Who Is the "We" We Yearn to Be?

This question is about identity and discernment. It is also about inclusion and recognizing a new "we" for what we might celebrate and rejoice. The Gospel and our life in Christ are not just for us but also for others. We need to create permeable circles of trust where others can enter in and change our circles. This can be a dilemma. We want things to stay the same and we want things to change. How to reconcile, make peace, or perhaps to discover new ground is often at the heart of the issue.

Elijah Anderson, a professor of sociology at Yale University, is one of the leading urban ethnographers in the United States.

He offers insights that might apply to the question: Who is the "we" that we want to be? We often live our lives in separateness even as we share community life in other ways. It's about the creation of space, and life within that space, that either has a particular people create it or is open for a diversity of people to create it. Despite our best efforts we are far from that creation of space that welcomes all who want to enter to have equal and viable opportunities to define the space. This has played out in other realities such as within Christian communities as we struggle with how to define our circles and at the same time welcome others in to change our circles. This issue does not mean that everyone needs to be the same, believe the same, or act the same. The richness of a wide canopy of religious expressions can be enlivening and renewing. It goes beyond race, ethnicities, economic and cultural status.

I live in a neighborhood where life is largely lived in backyards with high fences and where we all go in different directions for work. There is politeness exchanged but not much overall community awareness and depth. Our community is somewhat racially and culturally diverse, and there is little fear of crime. However, even when we might yearn to develop a new sense of who is the "we" that we yearn to be, it is not easy to attain. The exigencies of our lives make it difficult to know and bond with those who live around us. The question (who is the "we" we yearn to be?) may linger on for each of us as to how to engage it, and it will certainly be a defining question in our world for years to come.

This question, "Who is the 'we' that we yearn to be?" is not possible to be asked without risk in much of the world. People remain divided over faith, race, ethnicities, national boundaries, government policies, and a whole host of other reasons. But it can be asked by you and me and perhaps in the groups with which we affiliate and enjoy belonging.

Many years ago a person was asked about how to live his life in the in-between times between Christ coming into the world and Christ's return to the world in the end times. He responded that his journey was to live as though Christ reigned in his heart. And when that happens our point of view about life, others, and what it means to be a new "we" changes, expands, and transforms our lives.

Discernment is that capacity to see things not readily observed. Our identities are formed very early in life yet are still evolving. So we are all in a space where change is abundant even when we don't readily see or experience it. We know instinctively that change and structure are both essential for life. To have change and structure so inter-dependent and helpful for each to flourish is a lifetime challenge.

A number of years ago I wrote "Ode to a Teacher." Not technically an ode, but I wanted to discern what and who a teacher is that especially introduces us to new life and possibilities. In our Advent time and at the end of the day, hopefully we can take some time and wonder about the question of "Who is the 'we' we yearn to be?" as we contemplate the teachers or other significant people in our lives.

Ode to a Teacher

A teacher is one who learns. A teacher is one who leads us to a distant star and then joins us in the marvel of looking at the star in the first time sense of wonder, expectancy, and mystery. A teacher is one who recognizes that in teaching one another there is a learning that transcends traditional roles of teacher-student, without which the mystery of life cannot be entered into.

A teacher is one who listens. To hear and be sensitive to the sounds of silence means to tune into life itself: its questions, concerns, thoughts, feelings, comparisons, fears, anxieties, joys, securities or lack of them, and *pneuma* (the Spirit who gives life). The teacher who listens plows the ground for future crops.

A teacher is one who loves. To help another achieve new senses of identity, purpose, and meaning is one aspect of love. To forgive, to console, to touch, to heal, and to embrace those persons who feel unlovable is another. Teaching is running the race that is set before us; stopping for those who have fallen; and never starting for those who cannot run.

A teacher is one who laments. The lamenting teacher shows feelings and concern about brokenness in the world, not only willing to teach what he or she has read but also (most importantly) to teach what he or she has lived. Being open to cry over the hurts of others gives passion to the class, without which learning remains only superficial.

A teacher is one who longs. To wish, to hope, to dream, and to plan for new depths of existence heretofore unknown frees the teacher from giving yesterday's answers only to today's questions and instills in us a taste for the peace which passes all understanding. A teacher who longs has great potential for change and growth.

A teacher is one who lengthens. The teacher who stretches our imaginations, lengthens our reach for one another and for knowledge, and expands our possibilities of life is precious indeed. The teacher who lengthens ties into the mysteries of eternity itself and the eternal purpose of God.

A teacher is one who leads. The teacher who leads into charted waters but also runs the risk of leading into uncharted waters as well is invaluable. To lead without going too fast or too slow, to lead without being oppressive, and to lead with willingness to follow portrays one who is as concerned with the means as with ends. And alas, we find our ends in our means.

A teacher is one who laughs. To laugh at life and at one's self is to express a joy which though essential for life, the world is losing. To laugh is to comprehend and express the mysteries of life in a way that has no substitute. Laughing is the cry of the free—the forgiven—the redeemed. To laugh is to acknowledge the incomparable gifts of God.

As teachers lead us into new vistas and exploration we have the opportunities to imagine who it is that we yearn to be.

Reflect

1. Who is the "we" you yearn to be?
2. Who have the teachers been who have set your eyes on the future?
3. How can openness, difference, and change lead us to become ourselves to the fullest?

What Is My Vocation?

Our vocation is our response to a deeply felt mission or calling in life. That mission or calling can be expressed in a job or volunteer opportunity, an avocation, our family or friendship life, or in a myriad other places where we seek to make a positive difference in the world. Noted scholar and spiritual leader Henri Nouwen once said that a job is a temporary incarnation of a vocation. Gail Godwin, author and theologian, once said that vocation is that which makes more of us.

While on a boat in the Delaware River, I was asked if I could state my vocation in one sentence. I paused for a moment, asked if it could be a compound sentence, and responded: I believe my vocation is in response to God's mission in the world and my response is that I am called to help others learn how to fly and to fly. That has been with me ever since.

As I expressed my vocation, I centered it in the broader context of God's work in the world and my work of responding to that. It is not just a matter of druthers for me but rather a willing response to something much larger. The vocation I shared could be exercised in a number of ways. I am an Episcopal priest but also I am a man, a husband, father, grandfather, friend, colleague, photographer, storyteller, and encourager of others. My vocation as I thought about it in those brief moments and since then has been expressed in these various venues. I have been blessed by a wonderful family of origin, opportunities to learn and grow, and doors open for me to journey into different parts of the vineyard. I need not relish in that but rather work so that others might have a life less encumbered by the straitjackets placed upon them. You and I have some choices to make and my hope is that we both have as many as possible.

There are other ways we can discover our unique perspectives and gifts. Certainly asking others who know you to give their thoughts is an excellent way. An additional way I explored my vocation was to take the StrengthFinder Inventory[4] created by Gallup University. It helps identify fifty ways in which we exercise leadership and what our strengths might be. My results don't say how well I do exercise these gifts in various contexts but it does identify the priority of my leanings as I exercise my vocation. There are a variety of ways and inventories to help you identify your gifts and talents. Most of all, I encourage you to explore yourselves and claim what you discover.

Over the years religious institutions have often equated vocation with having a calling in the Church, such as ordination to the priesthood. No longer true, we have seen more clearly the vocational possibilities of each, of how that expression of who we are can be manifest in myriads of settings. Many of us hesitate to explore or claim our vocation, which can change over time. This exploration is our response to God and has been at the heart of billions of people from all faith perspectives. What is the mission of the God you worship? What are you called to do in response to that mission?

Throughout our lifetime we have the opportunity to explore our vocation in light of our changing circumstances. It is not a one-time-fits-all or a single opportunity at early moments of our living, but it is possible throughout our lifetimes. One of the ways we can do this is to observe and have conversations with persons of all age spectrums to discover how they seek to live out their lives. Life and the faith journey at its breadth and depth take us on a ride that winds its way in and through all the complexities and beauty of life. So when we reach one hundred years of age, we might indeed ask: What now?

A brief story about Herman, the uncle of my wife, Annie. He lived such an adventurous life filled with learning, scholarly research, and writing. He also liked to travel. And he also liked ice cream, always tasting new flavors with a gleeful smile. "I have never tasted that before," he would always declare. When he was in his early eighties he wanted to fulfill his bucket list by returning to Egypt. He invited Annie to go with him and they had a great trip. He even played the part of Pharaoh in a play as their ship cruised the Nile River. When he turned eighty I asked him, "Herman, what is it like to turn eighty?" He responded, "I can do everything I have always been able to do but only for five minutes!" He died as he lived, devoted to learning, exploration, and improving the human condition. But being a "people person" was at the top of his list, preceding everything else.

Reflect

1. What is that vocation, task, or mission in life for you?
2. What new ideas might you try on this week?
3. What is your "ice cream" of exploration?

Routines and Priorities

Bringing together many tasks into the present moment gives me the feeling that I am multi-tasking all the time. My propensity to cram too many things into a short day is still my practice, even in retirement where I have tried to rectify this by being present in the moment. Each morning I awaken early. I take out the dogs (a sheltie and a black lab) and have noticed they have a definite routine that doesn't vary much from day to day. I too have a routine; the early morning time seems to be my time for reflecting, being quiet, and preparing myself for the day. For some, that time might be in the evening when life might be a little more predictable. Whatever time it is, it seems important to have some routine to care for our lives in ways that matter most for us.

When I was younger my dad used to say there ought to be a time for doing nothing and letting the cares of the day go. When young, that seems to be possible if significant space is given between events and activities. Slipping back into that routine, whenever that may be, can be difficult in our world today, especially during Advent as we prepare for Christmas.

Routine can feel monotonous. Yet the setting aside for ourselves, that which replenishes us, can be ever so more salutatory. It is not so much doing the same thing at the same time every day, but rather doing what replenishes and sustains us every day. The routine can be in the hour of day or in the intention to create the space every day. We all have to work at intention. It is the time in this and every Advent season to pay attention to what feeds our soul and spirit. Perhaps a better question might be: What is it that our life revolves around?

The monastic communities share much wisdom in the structuring of their day around worship. It is worship that is front and center for them. In the Episcopal Church we most often celebrate Holy Eucharist on Sunday mornings. There are several alternative Eucharistic prayers and other parts of the liturgy that can have differences noted in the prayers and homilies highlighting the particular context of the day itself. Yet the day, times, and liturgies are routines upon which we build our week. Our lives are so full that regular attendance at Eucharist is now once every three or four weeks for some and Christmas and Easter for others. So resistance to routine may be even more prevalent in our society than we could have imagined. And our routines have changed to make room for new routines. But putting our priorities first should order our routines.

As we purchase gifts for others during Advent, it is important to think about what gifts to give ourselves. Stephen Covey shares a story that has circulated widely about priorities.[5] He stresses the need for us to differentiate the truly important from the merely urgent. Covey takes out a bucket (which symbolizes our life), a few big rocks (which symbolize our important priorities), and a bunch of small pebbles (which symbolize the urgent, busy tasks that aren't important). Pouring the pebbles into the bucket, he instructs an audience participant to try and fit in the big rocks afterward. It's impossible to do.

Then, Covey puts the big rocks into the bucket first, pouring the pebbles in afterward. The pebbles fill the cracks left between the big rocks, allowing the participant to fit everything into the bucket after all. One person in the audience raised his hand and said, "The point is, no matter how full your schedule is, if you try really hard, you can always fit some more things into it!" "No!" the speaker replied, "That is not the point. The truth this illustration teaches us is: If you don't put the big rocks in first, you'll never get them in at all."

Reflect

1. When is the time for you to prepare or reflect on your day?
2. In what ways might routine serve you? When is there too much routine or perhaps not enough? What is front and center for you in your daily routine? Is prayer or worship part of your daily routine?
3. What are the "big rocks" in your life?

Circling Back

One of the important lessons I have learned in photography is that the best pictures may be just behind me. I often get so focused on what lies ahead that I forget to look back. At this time in the Advent season, our thoughts, activities, shopping, and anticipation all look forward as Christmas is almost upon us. Could we slow down a bit today or this evening and look back at where we have come these three weeks? What have we observed? What have our prayers been about? Do you have new insights of your own or have you heard any from others?

I discovered an important perspective by commuting to work via train. I would often take the train from Trenton, New Jersey to New York City; trains were usually filled with occasional standing-room-only crowds. I found that if I had my back to where I was going, I could observe more clearly the surrounding countryside. If I faced forward, the countryside would come whizzing toward me at amazing speed. I gave up just a little bit of hesitation to gain a great deal in observation. This can be like our moving ahead with lightening speed toward Christmas—we might indeed miss what could be observed and learned if we did not look backward a little along the way.

What might we learn about ourselves, about Advent and this journey toward Christmas? What if we could pause, look around, and look back on where we have traveled? This is the rhythm of worship. We come from the valleys and highways of our life and intentionally become a part of a worshipping community. We begin by saying, "Blessed be God, Father, Son, and Holy Spirit," and its response, "Blessed be God's Kingdom, now and forever."

This is God's gift to us—this space and time. All life is a gift. We then give other thanks, ask for God's mercy, exclaim a *Gloria,* sharing again our thanks. Then we have some prayers and lessons for the day. A homily follows. Then a declaration of belief, more prayers for people and other concerns, a confession followed by absolution, and the exchange of God's peace. An offertory allows us to share the fruits of our work. Bread and wine are shared and blessed in the prayer for consecration to be the Body and Blood of Christ. This is done in the context of remembering the history of God's love and Jesus's Last Supper with his friends, ending with the Lord's Prayer.

We receive God into our very beings after hearing the "Gifts of God for the People of God." With additional prayers and singing all along the way, we are blessed again and dismissed to go forth to share life and good news with others—a gift freely given to all of us.

Affirmation, being valued and treasured, fed and nourished, recalling history and our place in it, being with others on the same human journey, opening ourselves to be nourished and empowered to be about our daily living—all of this and more in one hour's time. Eucharist, in addition to being all about thanksgiving, is about looking back to what has gone before us. Remembering how God has travelled with us throughout the ages.

It might be difficult to attend church in this season of Advent; we often have things to do, places to see, and a future for which to be prepared. It is often not until Christmas itself that we see others who have felt called to return to overflow the pews in our churches. But we who are baptized are already "church." The Advent season combines a sense of joyous hope in God's coming with the power in the fullness of time, as well as the radical call to look back and turn our lives around—again, that radical call of repentance.

In what other ways might our turning around benefit us? It helps us slow down. We can gain a three-hundred-and-sixty-degree perspective of life and ourselves when we slow the pace of our living so that hesitation might become rest. At these times we can experience how the whole world around us might become healing, and what seems like a relentless road forward can become an opportunity to enter a roundabout where we can reconsider where we are going and what we are doing.

Opportunities are inherent in a three-sixty review of the roads we are on. We can take the path we want and need to take. I remember driving in England and encountering my first roundabout. This juncture where several roads intersect offers several new possible roadways to travel. At first these roundabouts seemed very confusing, especially for Americans who are driving on the "wrong" side of the highway, but after a while I saw them as my friend. These roundabouts offered options to me including returning in the direction from which I came. This was especially helpful, as I often had taken the wrong turn before reaching the roundabout. It thus became an important juncture to gain my bearings.

It is also a place where we are reminded of the need to work for and with each other. When working with groups considering strategic planning, I often suggest that we loop around what we have already done so that we can more fully understand what has brought us to this point in our planning and to be open to other insights we may have missed along the way. There is always temptation for a group or individual to move forward with increasing speed to get the job done. I like to think of it as moving forward with deliberate speed, a speed that is informed by our past, cognizant of our present, and drawn into a future that is unfolding and revealing even as we speak.

The roundabout offers a helpful consideration of keeping on the same road or taking another one. You can go around the roundabout several times if you need to consider again your direction. In our travel through Advent, this pause might be just what we need to catch our breath, consider more fully what it is that we would like to do, and catch some wisdom along the way.

Reflect

1. What does circling around mean to you?
2. What do you see when you turn around and look behind?
3. How might it benefit you moving through these days as you seek to remain in the Advent mode of preparation and say grace over all that lies ahead?

Night

What Are the Possibilities?

Light and Shadow

The nights are longest at this time of year, and they often seem to be the darkest. The night opens up pictures that the daylight shuts out. Within our fears of the dark and the numbing sense that we may be losing our way, there comes the potential of light. It comes at night in many forms and from many places. At times it appears as the moon or the stars. At other times it is a sense of a new direction or perspective that shines internally within us. Yet at other times the light comes in our dreams which gathers our experiences, fears, hopes, and perspectives, and showers us with images of life and ourselves, never seen before. In any event, the night is not only a transition from one day to another but

107

also a resource that gives us rest, new visions, and quickened capacities to make meaning of our journeys.

I remember standing next to an outdoor fire in Taos, New Mexico a number of years ago, talking with family members and friends. I looked up and felt as though I was being drawn up into the complex of stars in such a way that even my feet felt elevated from the ground. I had seen stars before, but from that high-altitude perspective coupled with the breadth of the sky itself, I had never observed them in quite this way before. Context took on new dimensions for me that evening, and my mind was expanded in ways beyond my control and returned to me as a gift.

Of course the night can also be scary. It can contribute to our losing our way, and in our lost-ness be vulnerable to pain, fear, and suffering that the night only accentuates in our imagination. Night can hide others' dangerous intentions. At other times we can stumble because we cannot see the way forward or lose track of our bearings. At night we can feel very alone and lonely. We may yearn to go to sleep but cannot with our minds racing about the day behind or the day coming to us. It is at night when we are often exposed to the voices welling up within us—those still small voices that beckon us to holy ground or remind us of fearful places in our memories or psyche.

Of course, we know that we need the night. Without the night our earth would be scorched in heat, our activities would burden us beyond measure, our bodies and spirits would become weary, and the necessary renewal of life in all its dimensions would not be present. For sure many of us may rest and sleep during the day rather than at night, so night for those of us who work at night might, in some ways, have its generative effect available for us during the day.

Before the age of clocks, electricity, global communication, and so many other devices that remind us where we are at all hours, we had the night as instructor. There was a time when night meant retreat, no shopping, no TV shows, no church meetings; it was a time to gather with others and within ourselves so that we might be renewed in body and spirit and be safe.

As we contemplate the night and the various degrees of light and shadow that occur within these hours, we are also reminded of the gifts of persons who are physically blind. There is a sight that is beyond physical sight that illumines our journeys, informs our consciousness, and expands our understanding of what life in its depth and breadth is all about. While attending a meeting in a California hotel, I was sitting in the lobby and noticed that another meeting was also being held at that site. It was a meeting of persons who were blind. Small children were making their way through the hotel lobby to go outside on the warm, windy day. Watching them with their walking sticks, I noticed that many of them had a t-shirt with a special message inscribed: "I may have lost my sight but never my vision." I found myself transfixed on them and that message. All of us lose sight of where we are, who we are, or where we might be going. But to hold onto a hope that we might have a vision that sustains us is a real hope and resource indeed.

The way forward for those children in the lobby was made possible because they were helping each other and were assisted by sighted people with them. Their yearning was to enjoy the warmth of the sun and the coolness of the breeze; like all children, they were skipping through the lobby in their excitement. We are inextricably connected to one another at our best. When this happens, wisdom comes from all corners, strength is born anew, and our identity is deepened beyond our imagining.

At this point in our journey in Advent, it becomes difficult to maintain any semblance of patient waiting for Christmas. The need for Christmas preparations in their many dimensions is immense. The theme of the night might just offer us some respite from these activities and provide for us an opportunity to step back, if just for a moment, to reflect and be still. Perhaps this might be to "dream the impossible dream, to fight the unbeatable foe," but it just makes all the difference to us in our seeing our way forward.

Reflect

1. What does the night bring for you?
2. What brings light to your darkness?
3. What is the love of God that you might wish to be born in you this year?

In Search of Certainty

Today has the longest night. It is the winter solstice. Or is it? In the southern hemisphere it is the summer solstice, bringing with it the longest day. On this day as we reflect on life, we see that there are varieties of perspectives. For those of us who like to emphasize the positive, we may say that tomorrow will be a little brighter. Yet we know that brightness is not only a measure of physical sight but also an internal perspective about life. Brightness might just come to us in the dead of the night or in circumstances where we might not see readily our way forward. I am reminded again of the t-shirt worn by those blind young people that read: "I may have lost my sight but never my vision." Our vision can become a resource for us regardless of the light or darkness of the day.

111

In the Christian calendar, December 21 is the Feast of St. Thomas, often called the Doubter. Thomas, who questioned the presence of Jesus in his midst, was yearning to experience new hope after Jesus's crucifixion. He was skeptical in part because he was afraid of the vulnerability of affirmation when it might not become a reality. He was looking for certainty.

In *Wishful Thinking*, Frederick Buechner describes doubt as the ants in the pants of faith. It takes us to places of exploration, where, when engaged, we are kept on the edge overlooking certainty on the one hand and fearful, yet exhilarating questioning on the other. It is in this engagement of life that we are helped to incorporate change into structure and realize that we need both in order to survive.

Mystics, dreamers, theologians, philosophers, explorers—all have been informed by nighttime visions. They have encouraged us over the years to not be so afraid of the night, but rather see it as a resource. One of the journeys in life that we all take is a journey into mystery. Because the life around us is muted at night, it can feel mysterious, unwelcoming, fearful, and peaceful—all at the same time. It is a powerful reality in our life and helps, along with the sun, to provide a rhythm of respite, warmth and coolness, perspective, and an openness to the universe around us and within us.

Make no mistake; night can be a risky time. It is a time when certain types of crime are often committed, people become lost, and fear causes us to take risky chances—all often causing harm to body and spirit. In the midst of its resources and potential, there are real dangers lurking. The dark of the night can feel scary and place us in heightened vulnerability. So we must be somewhat cautious—maybe like Thomas who wanted some degree of certainty before moving forward. The dark of the night can also be a time of illumination as what is hidden by the light of day is available to us. During one of those times, I journaled the following:

It is now dark but I am trusting, hoping beyond hope, that the dawning of a new day is already being birthed. Maybe that is the hope, the promise. I have often needed some companioning getting there. So on this day I seek to dip into that well of memory and remind myself to help dig that well for others.

What can be certain and what cannot? Deep trust, enduring love, and openness to life in its depth and breadth can be anticipated by trusted companions and as we enter the realm of certainty. God's love, which knows no bounds and cannot be thwarted by any known or unknown power, can be experienced and believed to be certain. Certainty can be a guiding principle that grounds us just enough so that we can enter the world, which is decidedly uncertain.

It is often said that there are only two things that are certain: death and taxes. I believe that as long as we have life on this planet, we also have other certainties: birthing, growth, change, love, creativity, forgiveness, passion and compassion, repentance, hope, and promise. Of course these certainties do not present themselves in our every moment but are possibilities in many moments throughout our life. In the end we may feel that all we have left is hope. Waiting for the unknown, in darkness or light, provides room for possibilities. Advent can shout out: That will be sufficient!

Reflect

1. How can we be open to be embraced by these possibilities and share them with others?
2. How do we live creatively and hopefully between certainty and uncertainty?
3. Where is God in all of this for you?

Darkest Before Light

Someone once said to me, "It is darkest before it gets light." Sometime in the night that darkest place occurs. When it does it can seem as though it will last forever. We can gain some footing by looking up at the stars, those far-off suns that, from incredible distances, can grace our midst with beauty and light that can catch our imaginations like none other. It is in this space that I realize I can see things that have been blocked by the light of the sun: special plants that glow in the dark, the full range of the moon over a month's time, the incredible stars that draw me at times into their web, the lights and fires lit to provide warmth and direction. Yet something else happens. The dark can slow me down and draw me into myself, into dreams that inform, and into conversations that matter.

When I was a teenager I would sit on my parents' front porch or on the street corner of that quiet, relatively safe community talking with friends. It was often in the dark that I could sense their yearnings, fears, hopes, and dreams. It was in the dark where they did not have to prove themselves to others but could be real in ways that the pressures of the light made difficult.

Being in the dark requires some acclimation. The more we are in the dark, the more we can see what is around us and often what is occurring within us. We began life in the dark and will end life in the dark. As the Book of Common Prayer states: You are dust, and to dust you shall return. All of us go down to the dust; yet even at the grave we make our song: Alleluia, alleluia, alleluia (BCP 499).

How can we make the dark our friend? How can we receive the gift of darkness?

This fourth week of Advent, our image features a half-moon taken in the deep darkness of the night. It is important to hold our cameras very still at night so that the light can be most fully introduced to the lens without being blurred. A tripod helps. I also use a technique that involves breathing. As I am breathing out, and just before I have come to the end of that cycle, my body is the most relaxed. I then take the picture. In taking a photo of the moon, I find that it is helpful to have the exposure of the moon's surface buffeted by the dark. In that position I can see more clearly the contours of the moon.

Similarly the night can provide a contrast to the pictures that surround us and accompany us in our memories that help frame and illuminate them in special ways.

Being creative with our embrace of the night by seeing it in context to the day can ease the fear that may plague us from time to time. Stay with the darkness long enough to have its images unfold; let your memories or dreams be your companion beside you on the journey. The hope that we can embrace is that hope that nothing can separate us from the love of God. You and I can help fuel this hope by committing ourselves to one another along the way.

Most of us have been in what we might call the darkness when our way forward is not clear at all. But we have survived and even seen the insights that have come out of the darkness. This is a gift we can give our younger companions who may see present darkness in terms of "all is lost." The darkness does not need to overcome us, but rather can be a gift to us and to others.

The value of having hope cannot be understated. The lack of any hope is debilitating. But hope in what? We may come to terms with not having hope that a particular situation may turn around. Or we may understand that peace is not possible at this time or that reconciliation will not come any time soon. It is when there seems to be no hope on any horizon that life becomes despairing. We can make a difference in someone's life by being a beacon of hope to him or her. It may be encouraging them to sit still long enough to draw into clarity that which borders on light and total darkness, rest in that place, and begin to see that life in its fullness is both light and darkness and that you are companioning them along the way. Never underestimate the power of presence and love that will not quit.

As the nights are at their darkest, we know we have hope in new life, new birth, in Jesus.

Reflect

1. How do you experience darkness? How might you think of darkness as a gift?
2. In what ways is the night a gift to you? In what ways is the day a gift to you?
3. What learnings might come to mind as you experience darkness?

A Pentecost Presence

It was on a Friday before Pentecost in the year 2001. I left from my office on Second Avenue, walking the mile-and-a-half to Penn Station to take the train to Trenton, New Jersey, with four bags in tow, as I could not get a cab that day. By the time I got to Penn Station, I was tired and sweating. Pennsylvania Station is a huge hub of transportation for New York City with over 600,000 commuter-rail and Amtrak passengers a day. One never knows what track your train will come on, so the question for me was this: Would it come on a high-numbered track or a low-numbered or, perhaps, in the middle range? I know why I do not play the lottery, as I always seem to guess wrong. It happened on this day as well. I guessed low and the train came in high, so making my way to the entrance of the train platform, it seemed to me that the crowd numbering in the hundreds were going down the escalator in ways that resembled lemmings going off a cliff. I don't know what goes through the mind of a lemming but I believe that we all wanted to get down on that platform and on the train to get a seat. As I dragged my four bags (guessing yet again the wrong track number) I finally boarded the train to find there was no seat available. I put my bags down and found a small wall on the center of the car to lean on. Then came this announcement: "Ladies and Gentlemen." When you hear such an announcement you know there is going to be "bad news." A broken-down Amtrak train and a very slow moving NJ Transit train were moving in front of us. This was going to be a very slow trip.

A standing passenger's answer to prayer, we finally arrived at Princeton Junction, where a lot of people get off the train. I finally got a seat, sat down, and shortly discovered how quickly my body indicated to me that I was exhausted. When we finally arrived in Trenton, I grabbed my bags and exited the train. Still irritated, people were pushing their way past me and running off. I went to the escalator, only to discover it was broken, so I took to the stairs. The stairs are at a forty-five degree angle with a merciful platform halfway up. As I picked up my bags a young man approached me, offering to pick up one of my bags. I brushed him off at first, as I was now determined to carry them up the stairs myself. But he insisted. I gave him my biggest bag. He bounded up the stairs and waited for me. When I got to the platform at the top of the stairs he handed me my bag, smiled, and bowed. I smiled and bowed back. We didn't speak. I then realized he was deaf.

On the top of the platform that day I experienced three things: (a) What that young man did helped erase the stress of the long trip; (b) I was grateful I got on that train so I could meet him; and (c) On this Friday before Pentecost I had just experienced Pentecost. Pentecost, that wonderful mystery where the Spirit of God was present in such a way that people could understand others from other lands and tongues.

The remembrance of this event comes back to me on this day, six months apart from Pentecost. In Advent we are often rushing to yet other destinations, seeking to push back others who may be in our way, often experiencing a long, difficult journey wherever we try to travel. And yet we may just have amongst us another person who is not caught up in the rush of life and is waiting to provide assistance to others or us.

In the midst of our rushing around to buy a present, we may encounter another present that will be life-giving. Sometimes we discover this by needing help. At other times we discover it when we look for it. And, as it was for me, the present can come as a surprise.

Reflect

1. When have you encountered difficulties on a journey that has left you exhausted? How have you "survived"?
2. How has a stranger ministered to you? Have you ever helped a stranger?
3. Where have you found a surprise during this last week of Advent?

Let It Be

There is a prayer found in *A New Zealand Prayer Book* for Night Prayer, a service that is often called Compline which occurs at the end of the day. Its purpose is to help us conclude our day and prepare us for a quiet night.

> *It is night after a long day.*
> *What has been done has been done;*
> *what has not been done has not been done;*
> *let it be.*[6]

One of the most difficult things for many people is to "let it be." It is hard to get to sleep when our mind is racing with what if . . . , what now . . . , only if . . . , or what next . . . . I suppose one of the deep motivators is fear—fear of loss, looking foolish, what is to come in the morrow, or not completing a task that we might have really wanted to accomplish. At other times our minds just keep on keeping on and we don't really know how to slow them down. It is over the next few days that our coping skills might get most frayed.

Although the days are now getting longer, there is still a lot of darkness. Since the fall, the decrease in daylight hours may be taking its toll on people who struggle with a lack of sunlight. All of these factors including the stresses of the season that lead up to Christmas can keep us awake longer than we would like. This is a season where our memories run deep, our losses seem to linger, and expectations of ourselves run high.

We are now in a full slide toward Christmas where our greatest personal losses meet our greatest gains. It is the day where Christians realize yet again that God values all human life and sees our lives as significant even when we don't. This will be the day when God closes the distance between God and humanity and between all humanity itself. Of course, we don't fully realize or live into this truth, but it is true nonetheless.

This reality of God's love is also evident in other times and seasons of the year. It is a rhythm of our common life. Impending danger or darkness, whether on the outside or inside of our lives, can keep us up at night.

What might we do to let the quietness of our peace enfold us and let the fears of the darkness of the world and of our own lives rest in God? This is God's day of declaration, spawning new birth and reconciliation, demonstrating incalculable love and forgiveness, restoring and making new all creation. How is it that we can let go of any perception of the need for perfection, "getting it right," or "should haves" and be offered to God? I like the expression: Perfection divides us; brokenness unites us. None of us are perfect and the striving to be so is futile. But we can seek to be whole, and in our wholeness we experience brokenness. That, in part, is what is means to be a human being. Yet even in our brokenness all does not need to be lost. In our brokenness God comes into our lives in so many ways, particularly through other human beings. Each of us is on a quest for meaning, wholeness, peace, love, connection, and wanting to make a positive difference in the world.

We can look at the world as a "glass half empty" or a "glass half full." At this point in our season of preparation, choose to see life—with the help of God and others—as "half full." It can help us see the day, others, and life itself as generative, wondrous, and beautiful beyond measure. Not always easy to do. Changes in perspective often come slowly and in small measures. The good news is that over time these small changes actually change everything. Might this be so for you and for me.

Reflect

1. What is that yearning dwelling within you that wishes to be expressed through you?
2. How can you be sensitive to others in ways that welcome their expression of that yearning for themselves?
3. What does it mean that God closes the distance between us, and what implications does that have for you in the way you seek to live out your life?

Last Day

We come together to remember, to be reminded, and to be open to be surprised. We have been here before at this precipice connecting Advent with Christmas. We live in the world that largely knows nothing about Advent, so this precipice may have been new to you or has come earlier than you expected, if it has come at all. In any event we have reached another transition moment.

When I was a young boy we often decorated our Christmas tree on Christmas Eve. I don't remember marking Advent as a family, but we did see Christmas as a unique celebration that was enhanced by letting it flood down upon us. Our tree always stayed up until Epiphany, the sixth of January. So we had a full twelve days of celebrating Christmas. Our tree was always a tall skinny tree, just what my mother always wanted. As I grew older I became fond of the skinny trees as I could see through them, finding all kinds of places to hang bulbs, lights, and streamers.

Our ritual on Christmas Eve was to put out a cup of eggnog and some cookies for Santa. I had a taste of them before they were placed on the table, just to check out if they tasted okay. We went to bed and waited until the morning. On Christmas morning I would awaken my parents, along with my sister. My dad would go downstairs first, whistle a signal that the coast was clear, and that something special had happened overnight. We would then go down the stairs to see what special surprise awaited us, usually one special gift from Santa and a few other presents from cousins and friends.

Reflecting back on those Christmas Eves and Christmas mornings, I could gradually see that my dad was acting as a scout—one who goes ahead and says that the coast is clear and we can explore this new space. The gifts themselves were wonderful over the years but the special gifts were our being together and listening for Dad's whistle. I began to understand the gift that was the most wonderful gift was the gift of God's Son—to be one of us. And as the years unfolded that gift has multiplied in so many ways and locations.

When I left my work at the Church Center, I shared the news with a dear friend whom I had met several years before. I walked by him regularly where he worked on one of the corners in the City, and he became a prayer partner with me. When he learned I would no longer be visiting him on a regular basis, he stood up from the grate upon which he was sitting, looked up at the buildings around us, and tears gathered in his eyes. He then said, "It will be okay because God closes the distance between us. God closes the distance between us and between God and us."

This is the meaning of the incarnation—God became flesh and dwelt among us. This is the whistle signal that says the coast is clear and you can now enter the new space of discovery of life at its depth and breadth. This is the signal that the stable in which God brings about new birth is not only that stable or cave in the story of the birth of Jesus, but also that we are the stable in which God brings about new birth.

We began our sojourn into Advent wondering about significant questions in our life. Questions such as: Who am I? Who are you? Who are we? Whose are we? Who is the "we" we yearn to be? What is our vocation in life? How do we proceed? How do we know we are proceeding? Are we there yet? These questions are important as they deal with our identity, relationships with others, our vocation, our engaging mission and ministry, and how we reflect on how we are doing and where we are. These questions are poignant ones with which to engage in a season of preparation for remembering and living out again the gift of God to us, as well as contemplate what gifts we might share with one another. This Advent we have sought to encourage the exploration of these and other questions and to take seriously our human experiences as a window into discovery of the unfathomable riches of God's grace and the created order.

And yet one more important question to be asked: To whom do we give the power to tell us who we are? The answer to this question has competing voices in our world. As a result of Jesus's birth and God's seeking to bring new birth through you and me, is that we (humanity) are of inestimable worth to God. And, if that is true in God's sight, it should be apparent to each of us. The surprise is that God continues to want to work through you and me to do God's bidding of forgiveness, healing, reconciliation, justice, mercy, and love in the world. We are about to be summoned to enter the fray yet again. Are we open to do it?

Reflect

1. What Christmas traditions do you celebrate?
2. How do you experience the incarnation in your daily life?
3. To whom do you give the power to tell you who you are?

Conclusion

In Continuance . . .

I have always enjoyed and benefitted from the church year. Each aspect of the year focuses on an aspect of my journey—spiritual, emotional, relational, financial, physical, and vocational. All of these opportunities and challenges are part of our daily living, but it is good for me to be able to get off the dance floor for a bit to see life and myself from a different perspective. I am in the present moment, but in that present I am reminded that a past has preceded it and a future is beckoning. So I seek to remember the past, be reminded in the present, and be open to be surprised in the future.

I need to take this journey over and over again as life is complicated and life events may lead me to be stuck in those realities of time when the transformation I yearn for is a blend of each. Peter Yarrow (of Peter, Paul, and Mary fame) once shared with a group about leadership in music: It is important for a leader to know when to lead, when to blend, and when to follow. I am surrounded by books, memories, pictures of time past, as I am simultaneously immersed in the issues of the present, while dreaming about the future. In my daring to offer leadership, I am aware of the importance to step forward, to join the steps of others, and to look for new steps to follow.

Long ago on a roadside in West Virginia, my dad and I were waiting for a ride. I was getting anxious, as it was soon to be dark. He shared that he had been scared before and assured me that we would get home. He then said, "Buddy, you have to be somewhere. This is where you are now. Let's look around and see what we can see." A stream of water coming off the cliff became a waterfall. A flower by the railroad track became for me a garden. He shared with me resources from the outside and ones that were waiting for me on the inside. And I have never been quite the same again.

Life is not just about me but also about history, present realities, future choices—about others, the created order, and decisions that will affect generations to come, learning from the past. Søren Kierkegaard said that we understand our lives by looking backward, but we live them by looking forward. All of this and more is why I love Advent.

As I move forward I am reminded yet again of precious people struggling in grinding poverty and often being victims of prejudice and discrimination. I am reminded of people of all ages being abused in physical and emotional ways. I am reminded of people who are living on the streets and on the margins of life who often have little or no hope for the future. I am reminded of the victims of crime and those who commit crimes; the havoc all of this wreaks on human beings, families, friends, and society as a whole. I am reminded that we are part of a global village as never before, and what we all do affects all of us in profound and lasting ways. I am reminded that religious and faith affiliation is in flux and that the people of the planet struggle with the choices of pulling back and circling the wagons or opportunities to build bridges and deepen our commitment to one another and to the planet. I am reminded of these things and so much more.

And yet this does not stop me from wanting to try to understand my life by looking backward, to live as fully as I can in the present moment, and to seek to live my life looking forward in hope. May all of these things and more be in your quivers and satchels as you step yet again into the future. May we all remember and be thankful to hear and know those words wonderfully shared with me by a friend who lives a part of his life on a corner in New York City: It will be okay because God closes the distance between us.

Our journeys and questions are ever before us as will be other Advent moments.

Notes

1. http://efm.sewanee.edu
2. http://www.belovedcommunity.info/faith/faithfulmoderates
   /marksoftheliberatingcommunity.htm (Accessed March 3, 2015)
3. Letty M. Russell, *The Future of Partnership* (Philadelphia: The
   Westminster Press, 1979), 108.
4. http://www.gallupstrengthscenter.com
5. Stephen Covey's metaphor can be viewed here: http://www
   .youtube.com/watch?v=fmV0gXpXwDU (Accessed March 5,
   2015)
6. Anglican Church in Aotearoa, New Zealand, *A New Zealand
   Prayer Book* (San Francisco: HarperCollins, 1989), 184.